M. Cooke

Literacy Trios

EASTER

FRANCES MACKAY

HOPSCOTCH
EDUCATIONAL PUBLISHING

Contents

Page 65: 'Daffodowndilly', taken from *When We Were Very Young* by A A Milne, is reprinted by kind permission of Methuen Children's Books (a division of Egmont Children's Books Limited).

Introduction

▲ About the series

Literacy Trios is a series of books aimed at developing literacy skills using activities based on useful and relevant Primary Curriculum themes. The unique feature of the series is the provision of three differentiated photocopiable sheets for each activity within the books. This considerably reduces teacher preparation time by enabling the teacher to cater for three different levels of ability for each activity.

▲ About this book

Easter contains exciting and purposeful activities based on an Easter and Spring theme. It aims to:

- ▲ develop children's literacy skills through experience of a wide range of activities that concentrate on word, sentence and text level skills;
- ▲ support teachers by providing time-saving differentiated resources;
- ▲ develop the children's knowledge and understanding of Easter customs and traditions;
- ▲ encourage enjoyment and curiosity as well as developing skills of interpretation and response.

▲ How to use the book

The book has been designed so that teachers can 'dip into' it and use any activities that are relevant to the classroom work already planned for Easter. Alternatively, the teacher can use the activities to plan a whole unit of literacy work, based on an Easter theme. The activities include important historical and factual information necessary for understanding the customs and traditions of Easter time, as well as more 'fun' activities such as puzzles and games that children so enjoy.

Broadly, the activities could be used across the whole Primary age range in the following way:

- ▲ Activity sheet 1 – Infant level (P1–3)
- ▲ Activity sheet 2 – Years 3–4 (P4–5) levels
- ▲ Activity sheet 3 – Years 5–6 (P6–7) levels

However, as ability levels vary across age and class ranges, it is up to the teacher's discretion to decide on the appropriate activity sheet for individuals in their class.

Alternatively, the activity sheets could be used within one class to cater for the wide range of ability levels often present.

Published by Hopscotch Educational Publishing Company Ltd, Althorpe House, Althorpe Stree, Leamington Spa CV31 2AU.

Written by Frances Mackay
Illustrated by Cathy Gilligan
Cover design by Blade Communications
Cover illustration by Katy and Lizzie Warham
Printed by Clintplan, Southam

Frances Mackay hereby asserts her moral right to be identified as the author of this work in accordance with the Copyright, Designs and Patents Act, 1988.

ISBN 1-902239-22-9

Finding out about Easter

Name ____________________

The Easter festival

▲ Use the pictures and words below to answer the questions.

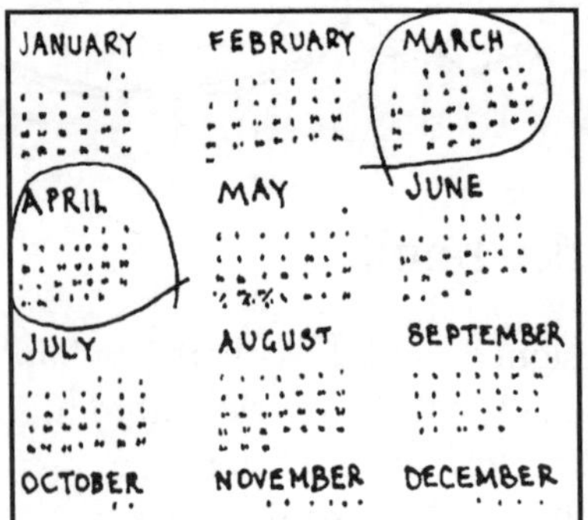

March or April

Jesus

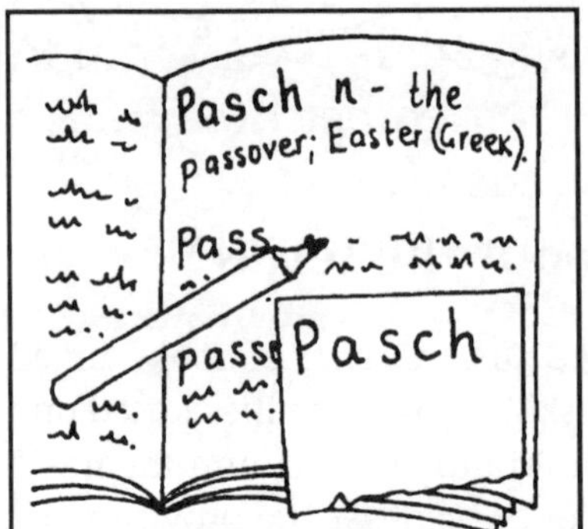

Pasch

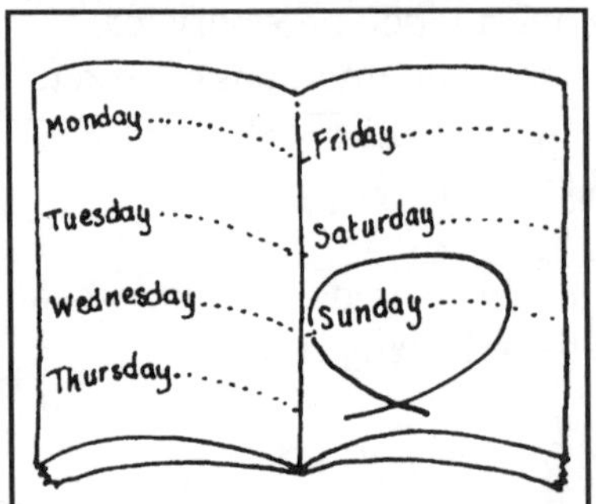

Sunday

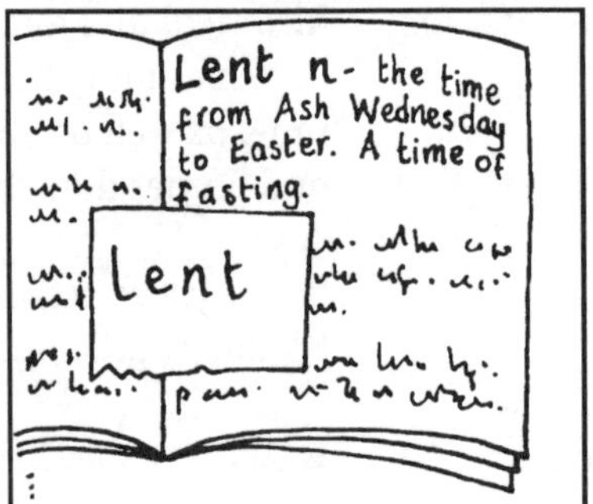

Lent

Mother's Day

1 In which months can Easter fall? ____________________

2 Whose death is remembered at this time? ____________________

3 What is another name for Easter? ____________________

4 On what day of the week does Easter begin? ____________________

5 What are the forty days before Easter called? ____________________

6 What special day is it on the fourth Sunday in Lent?

____

Finding out about Easter

Name ______________________

The Easter festival

▲ Read the following information about Easter.

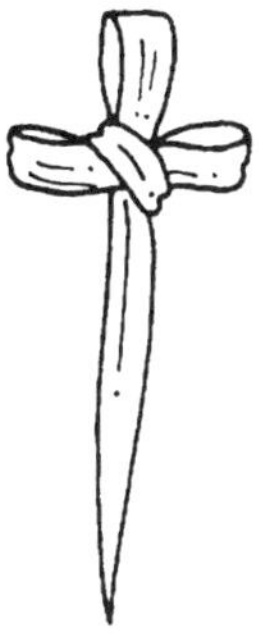

Easter is a very important Christian festival. At Easter, Christians remember how Jesus died on the cross and came back to life again. Easter occurs in spring in many countries so it is seen as a celebration of new life for animals and plants as well as for Jesus.

The name Easter may have come from the word *Eastre* which was the name for a goddess of spring. In many countries in Europe, the word for Easter is *Pasch*, which is a Greek word which means Passover.

Easter can fall between March 22 and April 25. The 40 days before Easter are called Lent. Other special days during Easter are:

Shrove Tuesday – the last day before Lent begins.
Ash Wednesday – the first day of Lent.
Mothering Sunday (Mother's Day) – the fourth Sunday in Lent.
Palm Sunday – the Sunday before Easter.
Maundy Thursday – the Thursday before Easter.
Good Friday – the Friday before Easter.
Easter Sunday – Easter Day.

▲ Answer these questions.

What do Christians remember at Easter? ______________________

____

What name is used for Easter in many countries in Europe?

____

What does this name mean? ______________________

When does Easter occur during the year? ______________________

What are the forty days before Easter called? ______________________

What is the first day of Lent called? ______________________

What happens on the fourth Sunday in Lent? ______________________

____

Finding out about Easter

Name ____________________

The Easter festival

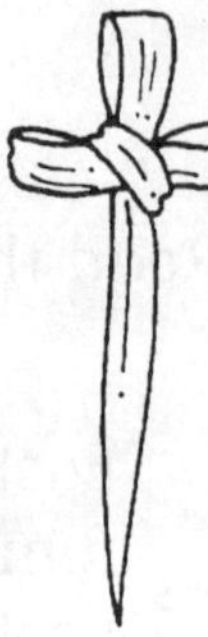

▲ Read the following information about Easter to answer the questions.

Easter is the oldest and most important Christian festival. It is the time of year when Christians commemorate the death and coming to life again (resurrection) of Jesus. Like most festivals, Easter has its origins in pre-Christian times when people celebrated the arrival of spring with its new growth of plants and birth of animals. Christians associate this new life in spring with the new life that was given to Jesus when He rose from the dead.

The name 'Easter' may have come from *Eastre* or Eostre, the name of a goddess of spring. The word for Easter in many European countries is *Pasch*, a Greek word that comes from the Hebrew Passover. The Passover is a meal eaten by Jewish people to celebrate the time when God rescued them from captivity as slaves in Egypt. The Passover is also the time when Jesus was crucified.

Unlike Christmas, the date of Easter varies. In Western churches, Easter Day is always on a Sunday, the Sunday following the first full moon after the Spring equinox. This means that Easter can fall between March 22 and April 25.

There are many special days during Easter and the 40-day preparations leading up to it, known as Lent:

Shrove Tuesday – the last day before Lent begins.
Ash Wednesday – the first day of Lent.
Mothering Sunday (Mother's Day) – the fourth Sunday in Lent.
Palm Sunday – the Sunday before Easter.
Maundy Thursday – the Thursday before Easter.
Good Friday – the Friday before Easter.
Easter Sunday – Easter Day.

▲ Answer these questions:

What do Christians celebrate at Easter? ____________________

____

What does resurrection mean? ____________________

Why do Christians associate Easter with the celebrations for spring?

____

____

What name is used for Easter in many European countries? ____________________

When does Easter occur? ____________________

What are the forty days before Easter called? ____________________

What is the last day before Lent begins called? ____________________

What is another name for Mother's Day? ____________________

What is Ash Wednesday? ____________________

When is Palm Sunday? ____________________

Finding out about Easter

Name ________________________

The Easter story

▲ Cut out the pictures and sentences. Put the pictures in the right order to tell the story. Match the sentences to the pictures. Stick the pictures and sentences on to a piece of paper. Make a border and write a heading. Colour it in.

Jesus is put in a grave.

Jesus rides on a donkey into Jerusalem.

Some soldiers arrest Jesus.

People cheer Jesus as he rides the donkey.

Jesus dies on the cross.

Jesus eats a meal with his disciples.

An angel tells Mary that Jesus is alive again.

Jesus gives the disciples bread and wine.

Name ______________________

The Easter story

▲ Cut out the pictures below. Put them in the right order to tell the story. Write a sentence underneath each picture to say what is happening. Stick the pictures and writing on to a piece of paper. Make a border and write a heading. Colour it in.

Finding out about Easter

Name ______________________

The Easter story

▲ Cut out the boxes below. Put them in the correct order as they appear in the Bible (King James I version). Use St Mark Chapters 11, 14 15 and 16 to help you. Fill in the missing words. Stick the boxes on to a piece of paper. Draw some pictures or a border. Write a heading.

Chapter 15, verse 46: And he (Joseph of Arimathaea) bought fine linen, and took him down, and ______________ him in the linen, and laid him in a ____________ which was hewn out of a rock, and rolled a __________ unto the door of the sepulchre.

Chapter 11, verse 7: And they brought the _________ to Jesus, and cast their garments on him; and he sat upon him.

Chapter 14, verses 46 and 53: And they laid their hands on him, and ________ him. And they led Jesus away to the _________ priest: and with him were assembled all the chief __________ and the elders and the _____________.

Chapter 11, verse 8: And many spread their garments in the way: and others cut down ____________ off the trees, and strawed them in the way.

Chapter 15, verses 25 and 37: And it was the third hour, and they ____________ him. And Jesus cried with a loud __________ , and gave up the ghost.

Chapter 14, verses 17 and 18: And in the evening he cometh with the twelve. And as they sat and did ________ , Jesus said, Verily I say unto you, One of you which ________ with me shall __________ me.

Chapter 16, verses 4 and 6: And when they looked, they saw that the stone was ________ away: for it was very great. And he saith unto them, Be not ____________ : Ye seek Jesus of Nazareth, which was crucified: he is ____________ : he is not here: behold the place where they laid him.

Chapter 14, verses 22, 23 and 24: And as they did eat, Jesus took _________ , and blessed, and brake it, and gave to them, and said, Take, eat: this is my ________. And he took the cup, and when he had given _________ , he gave it to them: and they all drank of it. And he said unto them, This is my ________ of the new testament, which is shed for many.

Name ______________________

Lent

▲ Choose words from the box below to complete each sentence so that it makes sense.

Lent	ash	called	word
days		like	pancakes

Lent is the name given to the 40 __________ before Easter.

Many people give up eating something they __________ during Lent.

The day before __________ begins is called Pancake Day or Shrove Tuesday.

The name 'shrove' comes from a ________ that means to forgive.

Many people cook __________ on Shrove Tuesday.

The first day of Lent is __________ Ash Wednesday.

In some churches today __________ is put on people's foreheads in the shape of a cross on Ash Wednesday.

Finding out about Easter

Name ______________________

Lent

▲ Choose words from the box below to complete each sentence so that it makes sense.

Wednesday	chocolate	forty	Tuesday	without
food	enjoy	during	cross	means
	burning	fasting	forgiven	put

Lent is the name given to the _________ days before Easter. The length of time __________ Lent reminds Christians of the forty days Jesus spent all alone in the desert without any _________ to eat. In the past, Lent was a time when people went __________ food such as eggs, meat and cream. Today, many people still give up something they ________ during Lent, such as ________________.

The day before Lent is called Shrove ____________ or Pancake Day. The word 'Shrove' comes from the word 'shriven' which _____________ to be forgiven. In the Middle Ages, people used up all the fats in their house before the forty days of ____________ by making pancakes. On that day, they also went to church to confess their sins and be 'shriven' or _________.

The first day of Lent is called Ash _________________. It gets its name from a custom begun when people wore clothes made from sackcloth and _____________ ashes on their head as a sign that they were really sorry for doing something wrong. In some churches today, the ash from the _____________ of last year's palm crosses from Palm Sunday is used to mark people's foreheads with a ___________ .

Finding out about Easter

Name ______________________

Lent

▲ Choose words from the box below to complete each sentence so that it makes sense.

filled	derived	burning	forty	Shrove	suggested	batter
forgiven	enjoy	wilderness	foreheads	cooking	Wednesday	
originates	year	confess	days	sprinkle	Tuesday	bowl
chocolate	without	century	eaten	house	Lent	means

Lent is the name given to the __________ days before Easter commences. No-one is quite sure where the word 'Lent' originates from but it may be ____________ from the Anglo Saxon word *lencten*, which ___________ spring or from the German word *Lenz*, which refers to the time of _________ when the days lengthen.

Traditionally, Lent reminds Christians of the time when Jesus spent forty ________ in the _____________ without any food. Lent therefore lasts for forty days. In the Middle Ages, Lent was a time of fasting. People went __________ food such as meat, eggs and cream. Today, many people still give up something they __________ during Lent, such as ______________.

In Britain, the day before Lent is called Shrove ____________ or Pancake Day. The word 'Shrove' ____________ from the word 'shriven' which means to be forgiven. In the Middle Ages, the people used up all the fats in their _____________ before the forty days of Lent by making pancakes. They also went to church on that day to _____________ their sins and be 'shriven' or _______________. Today, many towns and villages hold pancake races on __________ Tuesday. This tradition is believed to date back to 1445 in the town of Olney when a housewife who was late _____________ her pancakes, ran to church, taking her griddle and _____________ along with her! In some other countries, the day before _________ is called Mardi Gras or Fat Tuesday. In Sweden the food ____________ on this day is the Fat Tuesday bun which is _____________ with almond paste and whipped cream and is served floating in a ___________ of hot milk.

The first day of Lent is called Ash __________________. It gets its name from a custom begun by Pope Gregory in the sixth ______________. Pope Gregory ________________ that people should wear clothes made of sackcloth and should _____________ashes on their head as a sign that they were really sorry for doing something wrong. Today, the ash from the ____________ of last year's palm crosses from Palm Sunday is used to mark people's ________________with a cross in some churches.

Finding out about Easter

Name ____________________

Palm Sunday

▲ Use the pictures and words below to complete the sentences.

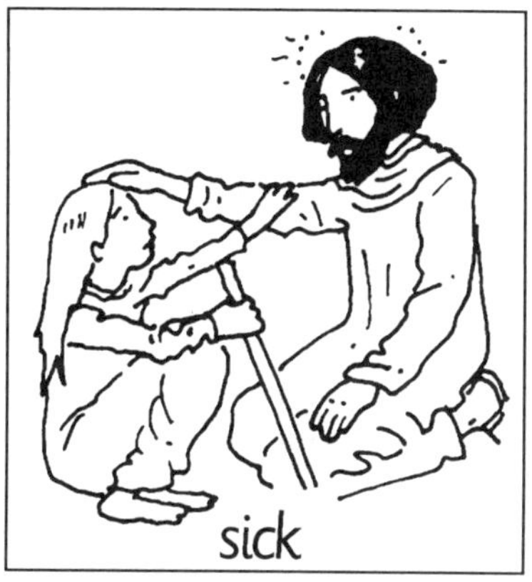

Jesus made ________ people well again.

Jesus told ___________ to tell people how to live a good life.

Jesus chose ___________ special friends to help him.

Many ___________ loved Jesus and went with him from place to place.

Jesus rode into Jerusalem on a ______________ for the Passover.

People were very happy to see Jesus. They lay __________ leaves down on the road in front of him.

Name ______________________

Palm Sunday

▲ Read the following information about Palm Sunday. Some important words have been underlined.

After Jesus spent forty days in the desert, he went back home to Galilee. There he began to tell the people about God and how they should stop doing wrong things.

Jesus travelled to many places. He became very well-known. He performed many miracles. The first one was at a wedding in Cana. The people ran out of wine and Jesus turned water into wine.

Jesus cared for people. He cured the sick and the lame. He made an old man see again and made a young girl walk again.

Jesus told people stories to help them understand how to lead a good life and be kind to others. He chose twelve special friends to help him. They were called the disciples. Together they travelled to many places telling people about God. Many people loved Jesus and followed him wherever he went.

After three years, Jesus and his disciples went to Jerusalem for the Passover Festival. Jesus rode on a donkey into Jerusalem. When the people saw him they cheered and some people broke off branches from palm trees and waved them like flags. They also put palm leaves down on the road before Jesus to carpet the way.

Today this day is celebrated on the Sunday before Easter and is known as Palm Sunday.

▲ Now use the underlined words to write some sentences of your own about Palm Sunday.

Finding out about Easter

Name ______________________

Palm Sunday

▲ Read the following information about Palm Sunday.
For each paragraph, circle three or four key words.

After Jesus had spent forty days in the wilderness, he returned to his home country of Galilee. There he began to tell the people about God and how they must turn away from their sins and believe in 'God's Good News'.

Jesus then travelled to many towns and villages. He became very well-known as a person who was always ready to help others. He performed many miracles, the first of which was at a wedding reception in Cana. When the wine at the wedding ran out, Jesus turned some water into wine.

Jesus also cured many sick people. He restored the sight of a blind man and made a young lame girl walk again. Jesus cured a man with leprosy and another man who was paralysed.

Many people began to follow Jesus because they believed in him. He told stories to huge crowds of people to help them understand how they could lead good and honest lives. These stories were known as parables. Of all his followers, Jesus chose twelve special friends to help him spread his messages. The twelve he chose were: Simon (Jesus gave him the name Peter), James, John, Andrew, Philip, Bartholomew, Matthew, Thomas, James the son of Alphaeus, Thaddaeus, Simon and Judas. These twelve people were called the disciples or apostles.

After many years of travelling, Jesus and his disciples joined the crowds going to Jerusalem for the Passover Festival. Jesus rode on a donkey into Jerusalem. As he entered the city, people flocked to welcome him. They cheered and broke off branches from palm trees to wave like flags. Some people laid the palm leaves down on the road before Jesus to carpet the way.

Today this day is celebrated on the Sunday before Easter and is known as Palm Sunday.

▲ Use your key words to write a summary of each paragraph. Make sure you include all the important facts about the events leading up to Palm Sunday.The Last Supper

Continue on the back of this sheet.

Name ______________________

The Last Supper

▲ Read this story about The Last Supper. Some words are underlined.

One day Jesus had a special meal with the twelve disciples. Before the meal Jesus put a towel around his waist and washed the feet of each person, instead of asking the servant to do it. Jesus did this to show that he was no better than anyone else and that everyone should be treated the same.

At the meal Jesus told his friends that he was going to die soon. He broke some bread into many pieces and said: 'Take, this and eat it, this is my body.' And then Jesus gave his friends some wine, telling them that the wine was his blood. The disciples felt very sad that Jesus was going to die.

Then Jesus told his friends that one of them was going to help some soldiers to arrest him and take him to the Roman leader. The disciples did not think this could be true but it did happen. It was Judas who told the soldiers where Jesus was.

▲ Use a dictionary to find out the meanings of the words underlined. Write the meanings here:

special ______________________

servant ______________________

disciples ______________________

arrest ______________________

Finding out about Easter

Name ______________________

The Last Supper

▲ Read this information about The Last Supper. Use a dictionary to write down the meanings of the words underlined.

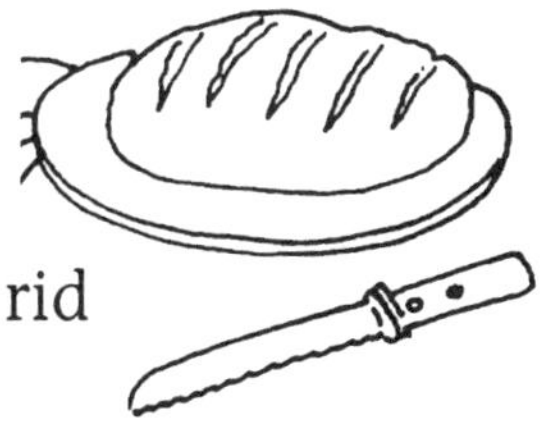

Two days before the Feast of the Passover, the chief priests and other important leaders were talking about how they could get rid of Jesus. They were jealous and afraid of him. Judas, one of the disciples, offered to help them arrest Jesus. The chief priests were very happy and paid Judas a reward.

On the evening before the Passover, Jesus shared a special meal with his disciples. Before the meal, he did something that amazed his disciples. He washed their feet. This was usually done by a servant but Jesus did this to show that everyone should be treated the same and that no task should be beneath anyone.

At the meal Jesus told his disciples that he was going to die soon and that one of them would betray him. Then he broke the bread into many pieces and gave the disciples some each. He said that the bread was his body. Jesus gave them some wine and told them that the wine was the blood that would be spilled when he died. The disciples were very sad to learn that Jesus was going to die. They did not want to believe that it was true.

Jesus tried to explain why he had to die and how he would rise again from the dead, but the disciples did not understand. Peter said that he would rather die than let this happen to Jesus. But Jesus shook his head sadly and told Peter that before dawn he would say three times that he had never known Jesus. Everything Jesus said would happen came true. This meal was the last one they had together before Jesus was crucified on the cross.

▲ Write the definitions of the underlined words here.

Passover ______________________

jealous ______________________

disciples ______________________

arrest ______________________

servant ______________________

betray ______________________

explain ______________________

dawn ______________________

crucified ______________________

Finding out about Easter

Name ____________________

The Last Supper

▲ Read this information about The Last Supper. Use a dictionary to write down the meanings of the words underlined.

The Passover is a celebratory meal which was first held thousands of years ago and is still eaten every year in Orthodox Jewish households. The Passover meal is a reminder of a time in Jewish history, recorded in the Bible in the Old Testament book of Exodus, when the nation of Israel was rescued from slavery in Egypt. On that night, God struck the firstborn Egyptian children with death but 'passed over' the Israelite households. After that, the king of Egypt let the slaves go free. The Passover meal reminds the Jewish people how God saved them from slavery and helped them.

The Bible tells us that two days before Jesus was going to celebrate his Passover meal with his disciples, the chief priests and important leaders were plotting to get rid of Jesus. They were aware that many people followed Jesus and they were afraid of his power. They agreed to find someone to spy on Jesus. Then Judas, one of the disciples, offered to help them arrest Jesus. The chief priests were extremely pleased about this and paid Judas a reward of thirty pieces of silver.

Before Jesus sat down at the Passover meal with his disciples, he did an amazing thing. He washed the feet of each person, a menial task normally performed by a servant. Jesus did this to show his disciples that they should never think anything they do to be beneath them.

At the meal, Jesus explained that he was going to die soon and that it would be one of the disciples who would betray him. He blessed some bread, broke it and gave it to each disciple, telling them that the bread was his body. He blessed the wine and told them to drink it, explaining that the wine was his blood that would be spilled when he died. The disciples were very upset and Peter said that he would rather die than let this happen. But Jesus shook his head and told Peter that before daybreak he would deny three times that he had ever known Jesus. All that Jesus said came true and Jesus was captured and crucified on a cross. This last Passover meal spent with the disciples is now called The Last Supper by Christians.

▲ Write the definitions of the underlined words here.

celebratory ____________________

Orthodox ____________________

nation ____________________

slavery ____________________

plotting ____________________

arrest ____________________

extremely ____________________

menial ____________________

betray ____________________

deny ____________________

crucified ____________________

Finding out about Easter

Name ____________________

Good Friday

▲ Use the words in the box below to complete this newspaper report.

friends	Jesus	asked	cross
stone	Friday	Mary	killed

The Easter Times

Jesus Dies on the Cross!

On __________ morning, Jesus was sent to the leader of the city, called Pilate. Pilate ________ Jesus lots of things but he did not think that _________ had done anything wrong.

Pilate asked the people what to do. They said that Jesus should be ________. So Jesus was taken to a hill and nailed to a _________ to die.

Jesus was put into a grave. A big ________ was rolled in front of the grave.

On Sunday morning a lady called __________ went to the grave. The stone had moved. The body of Jesus had gone!

Mary told her __________ that an angel had come to her and told her that Jesus was alive again.

Finding out about Easter

Name ______________________

Good Friday

▲ Use these notes to write a newspaper report.

- Friday morning – Jesus is taken to the Roman Governor, Pontius Pilate
- Pilate questions Jesus but does not find him guilty of anything
- As is the custom at Passover, Pilate has to set free one of the prisoners
- Pilate asks the people which prisoner they want set free
- The people want Barabbas to go free. They want Jesus to be killed
- Jesus is nailed to a cross and dies
- Jesus is buried in a tomb and a stone is rolled in front of it
- On Sunday Mary Magdalene visits the tomb. The stone has moved. Jesus has gone
- An angel visits Mary to tell her that Jesus is alive again

The Easter Times

Finding out about Easter

Name ______________________

Good Friday

▲ Write a newspaper report about the death of Jesus on the cross. Write about how Jesus was taken to see Pontius Pilate and how it was decided that Jesus should die. Describe how Jesus was nailed to a cross and how he was buried in a tomb. Explain how Mary Magdalene discovered that Jesus had risen from the dead. Use information books and the Bible (St Matthew, chapters 27 and 28) to help you.

The Easter Times

Name ______________________

Easter customs

▲ Match the picture to the correct word in this glossary.

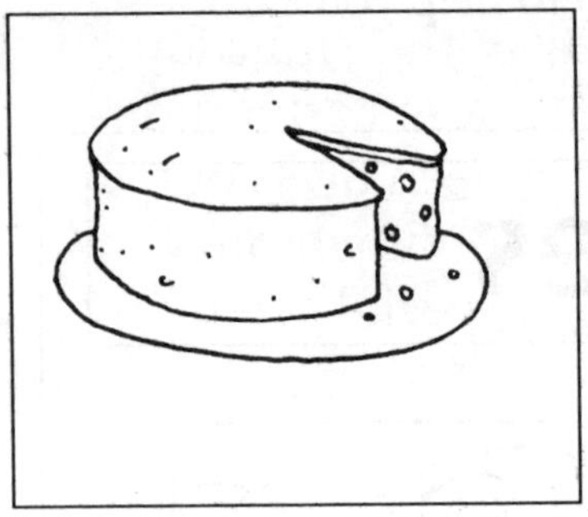

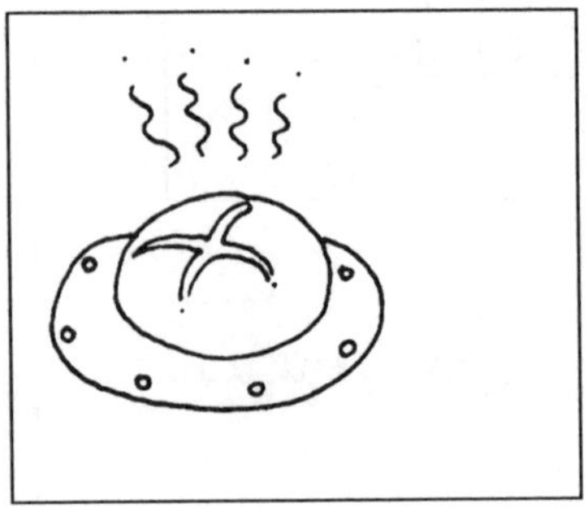

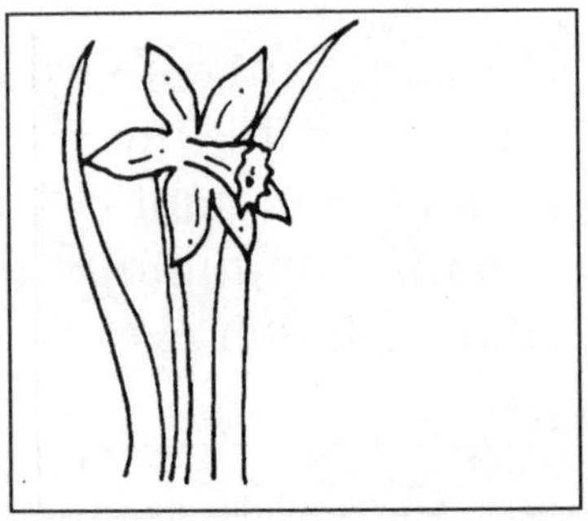

Glossary

Palm cross – a cross made of palm leaves

Pancake – a thin cake made from batter

Easter egg – a chocolate egg given at Easter

Simnel cake – a fruit cake eaten at Easter

Hot cross bun – a bun eaten at Easter

Mother's Day card – a card given to mothers on Mothering Sunday

Daffodil – a yellow spring flower

Easter card – a card given at Easter

Pancake race – a race held on Shrove Tuesday

Easter bonnet – a special hat worn at Easter

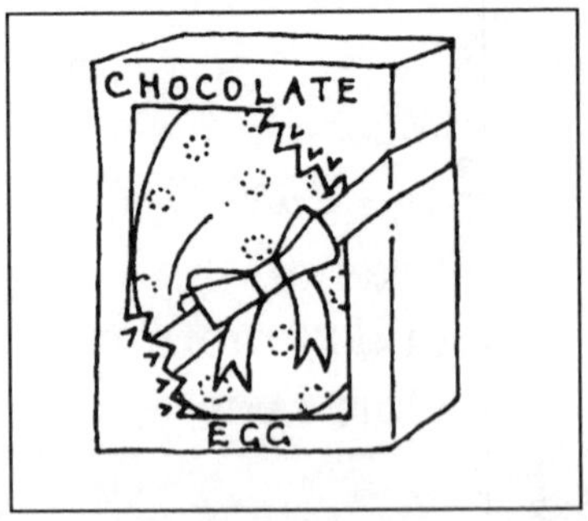

Name ______________________

Easter customs

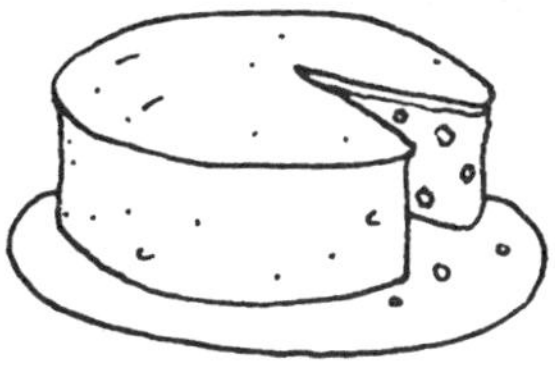

▲ Match each piece of writing to the correct word in this glossary.

On the Sunday before Easter, many churches give out palm crosses made out of palm leaves

In the sixteenth century girls would bake a simnel cake to give to their mothers on Mothering Sunday

On Shrove Tuesday many people make pancakes. In some places they hold pancake races

In the Caribbean the Mardi Gras begins with a rocket on the Sunday morning before Lent

In Sweden and Germany some people decorate their houses with an Easter tree

Glossary

Hot cross bun – a yeast bun marked with a cross

Mardi Gras – the festival/ carnival of Shrove Tuesday

Bonfire – a large outdoor fire

Palm cross – a cross made of palm leaves given out on Palm Sunday

Maundy money – specially minted coins given by the British sovereign on Maundy Thursday

Easter egg – a chocolate egg given at Easter

Simnel cake – a fruit cake covered with marzipan, eaten at Easter

Passion Play – a play about the Passion (sufferings) of Jesus from the Last Supper to his death

Pancake – a thin flat cake made from batter and fried on both sides

Easter tree – a small tree hung with painted eggs or dough figures used as a decoration at Easter

On the Thursday before Easter the Queen gives out Maundy money at a special ceremony

A huge Passion Play is held in Oberammergau in Austria every ten years

Traditionally, decorated hard-boiled eggs were given on Easter morning. Today, chocolate Easter eggs are usually given

On Good Friday it is the custom in many countries to eat hot cross buns

In some parts of Germany it is the tradition to light bonfires on hilltops during Easter eve

Finding out about Easter

Name ______________________

Easter Customs

▲ Match each piece of text to the correct word in this glossary.

On Palm Sunday, many churches give out palm crosses to remind people of how the crowd paved the road with palm leaves as Jesus entered Jerusalem

In the sixteenth century girls would prove their skills in the kitchen by baking a simnel cake to present to their mothers on Mothering Sunday. The word 'simnel' probably originates from the Latin word *simila*, a fine wheaten flour

Pancakes are traditionally eaten on Shrove Tuesday. The custom dates back to the Middle Ages when people would use up all the fats in the house before Lent began

In the Caribbean islands of Trinidad and Tobago the beginning of Mardi Gras is announced with a rocket on the Sunday morning before Lent, known as *Dimanche Gras*

In Sweden the Easter tree is made from birch branches and arranged in a vase, while in Germany it is made from a wooden cross covered in greenery

Glossary

Hot cross bun – a yeast bun marked with a cross

Mardi Gras – the festival/ carnival of Shrove Tuesday

Bonfire – a large outdoor fire

Palm cross – a cross made of palm leaves given out on Palm Sunday

Maundy money – specially minted coins given by the British sovereign on Maundy Thursday

Easter egg – a chocolate egg given at Easter

Simnel cake – a fruit cake covered with marzipan, eaten at Easter

Passion Play – a play about the Passion (sufferings) of Jesus from the Last Supper to his death

Pancake – a thin flat cake made from batter and fried on both sides

Easter tree – a small tree hung with painted eggs or dough figures used as a decoration at Easter

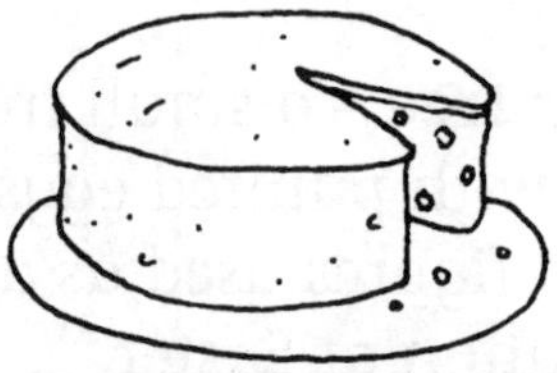

On Maundy Thursday, the British sovereign gives out Maundy money at a special ceremony. The clergy wear linen towels on their shoulders to remind people of how Jesus washed the feet of his disciples

A Passion Play is held in Oberammergau in Austria every ten years. The Play began in 1633 to thank God for protecting the people during the Black Death

Traditionally, decorated hard-boiled eggs were given on Easter morning. Today, chocolate eggs are usually given. For Christians, the egg is a symbol of Jesus' resurrection and new life

On Good Friday it is the custom in many countries to eat hot cross buns. Good Friday was originally called 'God's Friday'.

It is a tradition in some parts of Germany to light bonfires on the hilltops during Easter eve. People play games and sing hymns

Games and puzzles

Name ______________________

Easter words

▲ Look at these words. Write them in the box below in alphabetical order.

a
b
c
d
e
f
g
h
i
j
k
l
m
n
o
p
q
r
s
t
u
v
w
x
y
z

egg

bun

cross

Jesus

rabbit

pancake

flower

mother

donkey

lamb

Sunday

grave

Write the words here in the correct order.

1	5	9
2	6	10
3	7	11
4	8	12

Name ______________________

Easter words

▲ Write the following words in dictionary order.

bells	1	______
bunny	2	______
bonnet	3	______
bun	4	______
basket	5	______
bulb	6	______

cross	1	______
Christ	2	______
chicken	3	______
candle	4	______
chocolate	5	______
church	6	______

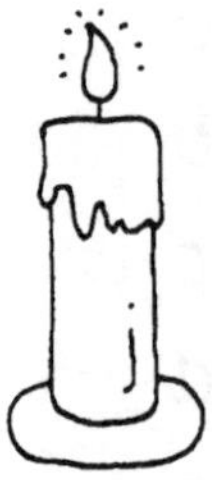

last	1	______
Lord	2	______
lamb	3	______
light	4	______
linen	5	______
Lent	6	______

Maundy	1	______
March	2	______
mother	3	______
Mary	4	______
money	5	______
Mardi Gras	6	______

Peter	1	______
Pilate	2	______
palm	3	______
pancake	4	______
Passover	5	______
parade	6	______

supper	1	______
Shrove	2	______
simnel	3	______
Sunday	4	______
service	5	______
stone	6	______

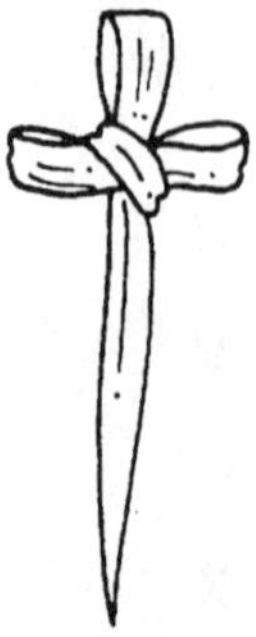

Games and puzzles

Name ____________________

Easter words

▲ All of these words have been used in an information book about Easter. Sort through them to make part of an index for the book. Make sure the words under each letter are in dictionary order.

Easter Sunday	Jerusalem	disciples	crucifixion	Good Friday
Last Supper	decoration	Judas	Lent	Ash Wednesday
Holy Week	kulich	bonnets	donkey	Eostre
lamb	April	cross	festival	grave
Jesus	carnival	holiday	Jews	hot cross buns
bread	chocolate	eggs	church	daffodil
dates	cakes	games	Lenten	customs

Index

A

B

C

D

E

F

G

H

I

J

K

L

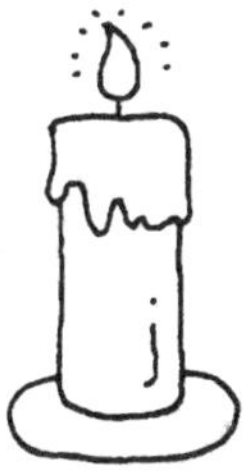

Games and puzzles

Name

Spring babies

▲ Match the animals with their young. Write their names.

Name ______________________

Spring babies

▲ Match the names of these animals with their young.
Use a dictionary to help you.

cat
cow
goose
fox
sheep
dog
butterfly
swan
deer
goat
kangaroo
pig
frog
duck
moorhen
owl
horse

piglet
kid
duckling
foal
tadpole
gosling
cygnet
joey
chick
kitten
lamb
caterpillar
calf
owlet
cub
fawn
pup

Games and puzzles

Name ______________________

Spring babies

▲ Write the name for the young of each of these animals. Use information books to help you.

dragonfly	____________	frog	______________
goose	____________	hare	______________
cat	____________	pig	______________
deer	____________	cow	______________
kangaroo	____________	badger	______________
goat	____________	elephant	______________
horse	____________	swan	______________
duck	____________	fox	______________
dog	____________	sheep	______________
lion	____________	butterfly	______________
seal	____________	rabbit	______________
bear	____________	whale	______________
trout	____________	eel	______________
bee	____________	pheasant	______________
squirrel	____________	eagle	______________
louse	____________	fly	______________
owl	____________	pigeon	______________

Games and puzzles

Name ______________________

Search the egg

▲ Look at the words in the chicken's list. Circle the words which are opposite in meaning inside the egg. One has been done for you.

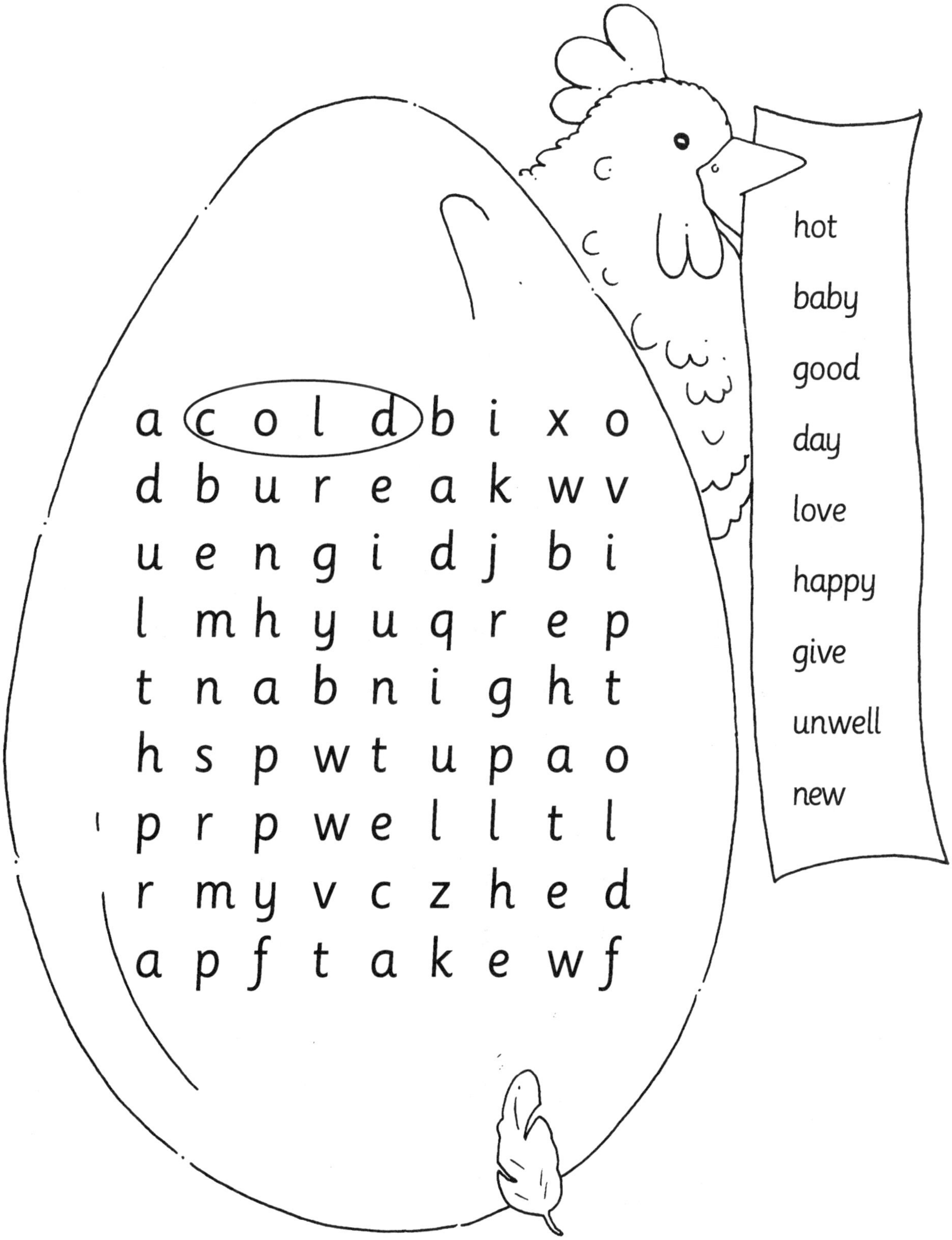

Name ______________________

Search the egg

▲ Look at the words in the chicken's list. Circle the words which are opposite in meaning inside the egg. Use a thesaurus to help you. One has been done for you.

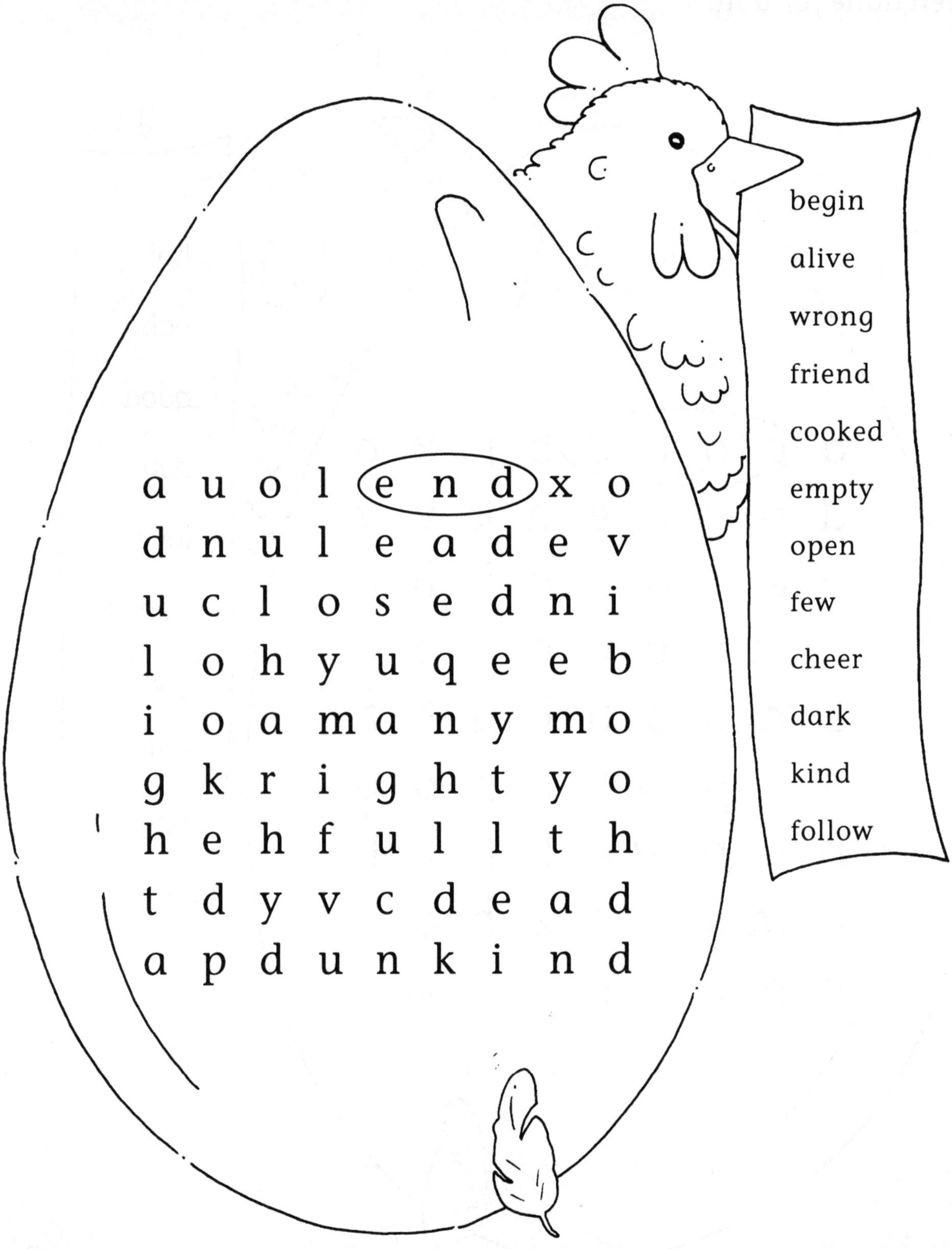

a	u	o	l	e	n	d	x	o
d	n	u	l	e	a	d	e	v
u	c	l	o	s	e	d	n	i
l	o	h	y	u	q	e	e	b
i	o	a	m	a	n	y	m	o
g	k	r	i	g	h	t	y	o
h	e	h	f	u	l	l	t	h
t	d	y	v	c	d	e	a	d
a	p	d	u	n	k	i	n	d

begin
alive
wrong
friend
cooked
empty
open
few
cheer
dark
kind
follow

Games and puzzles

Name ________________

Search the egg

▲ Look at the words in the chicken's list. Circle the words which are opposite in meaning inside the egg. Use a thesaurus to help you. One has been done for you.

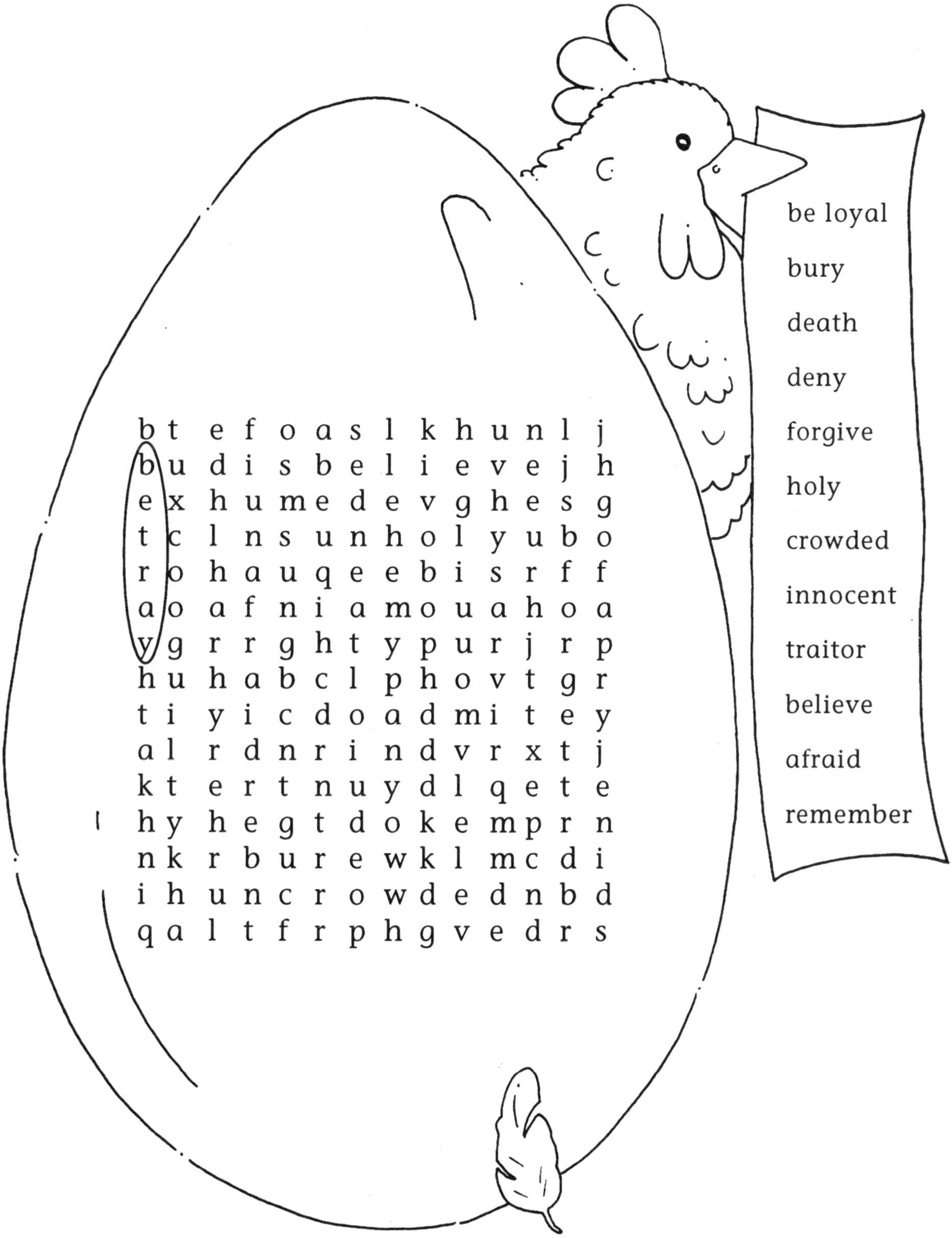

b	t	e	f	o	a	s	l	k	h	u	n	l	j
b	u	d	i	s	b	e	l	i	e	v	e	j	h
e	x	h	u	m	e	d	e	v	g	h	e	s	g
t	c	l	n	s	u	n	h	o	l	y	u	b	o
r	o	h	a	u	q	e	e	b	i	s	r	f	f
a	o	a	f	n	i	a	m	o	u	a	h	o	a
y	g	r	r	g	h	t	y	p	u	r	j	r	p
h	u	h	a	b	c	l	p	h	o	v	t	g	r
t	i	y	i	c	d	o	a	d	m	i	t	e	y
a	l	r	d	n	r	i	n	d	v	r	x	t	j
k	t	e	r	t	n	u	y	d	l	q	e	t	e
h	y	h	e	g	t	d	o	k	e	m	p	r	n
n	k	r	b	u	r	e	w	k	l	m	c	d	i
i	h	u	n	c	r	o	w	d	e	d	n	b	d
q	a	l	t	f	r	p	h	g	v	e	d	r	s

be loyal
bury
death
deny
forgive
holy
crowded
innocent
traitor
believe
afraid
remember

Name ______________________

Make the egg

▲ Cut out all the pieces. Use all the pieces to make an egg. Glue the pieces onto a piece of paper. Decorate the egg by colouring all the 'doing' words or verbs in red and all the other words in blue.

Name ____________________

Make the egg

▲ Cut out all the pieces. Use all the pieces to make an egg. Glue the pieces onto a piece of paper. Decorate the egg by colouring all the 'doing' words or verbs in red and all the other words in blue.

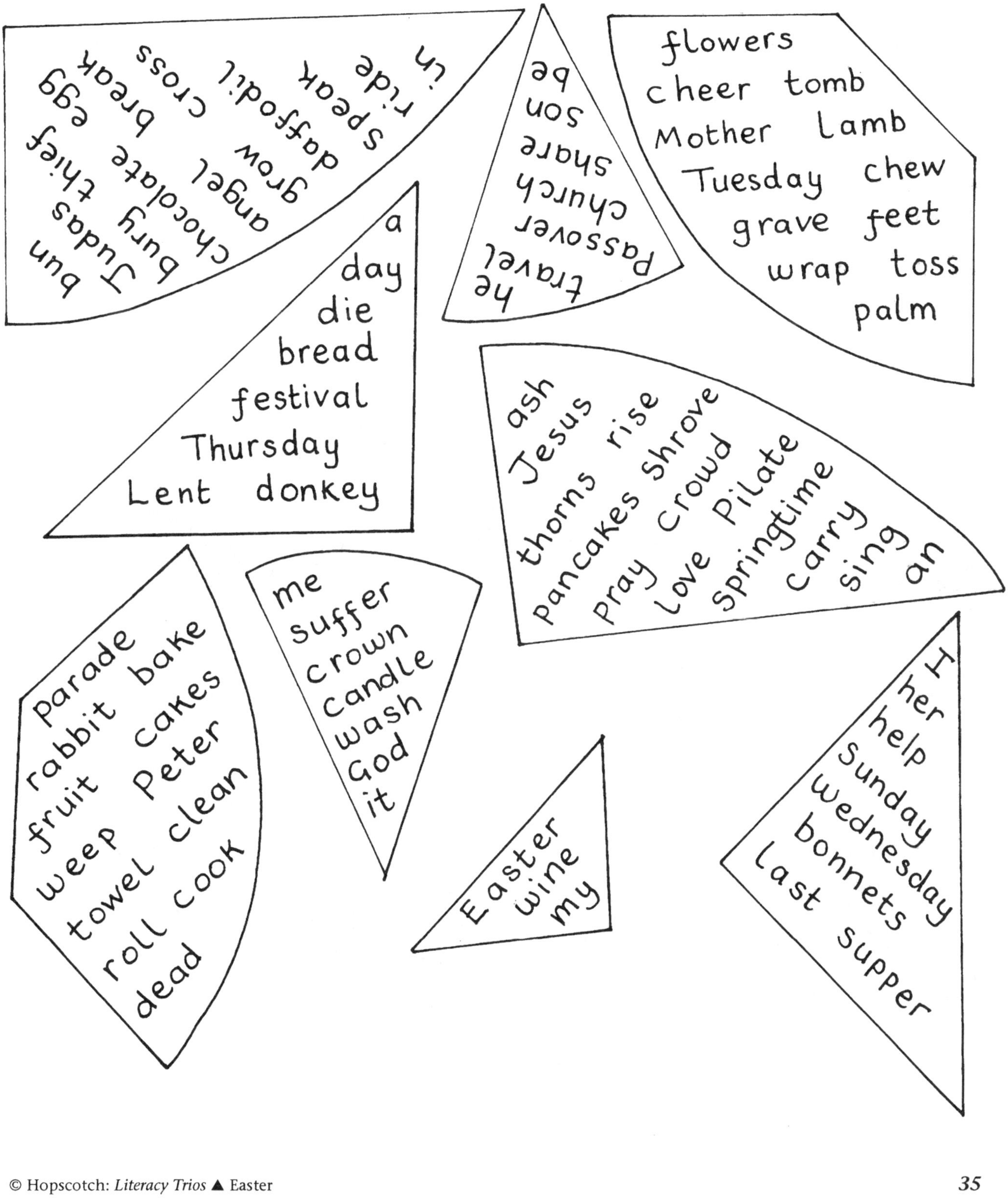

Name ______________________

Make the egg

▲ Cut out all the pieces. Use all the pieces to make an egg. Glue the pieces onto a piece of paper. Decorate the egg by colouring all the 'doing' words or verbs in red and all the other words in blue.

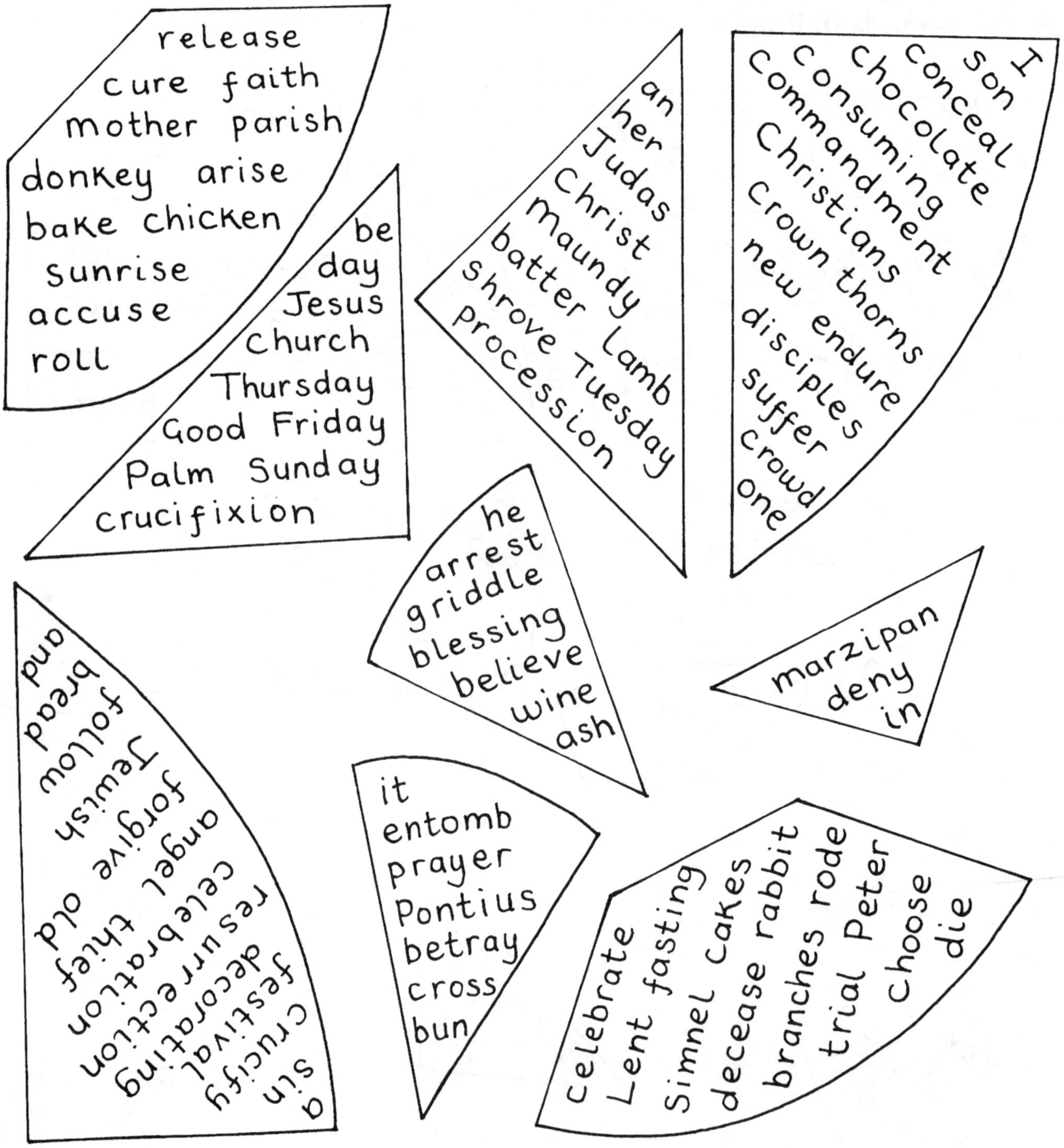

▲ Use a dictionary to help you find out the meaning of any words you do not know.

Games and puzzles

Name ____________________

Match the words

Some words are made up of other words, for example:
rainbow = rain + bow

▲ To work out the Easter words below, write the words to match each picture. Use a dictionary to help you spell the words. The first one has been done for you.

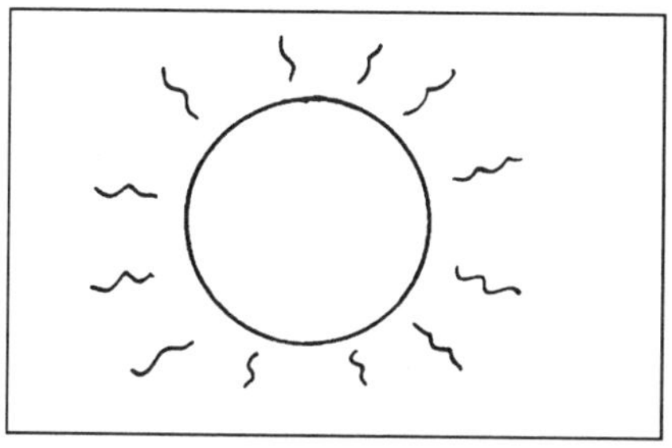 + 

Sunday

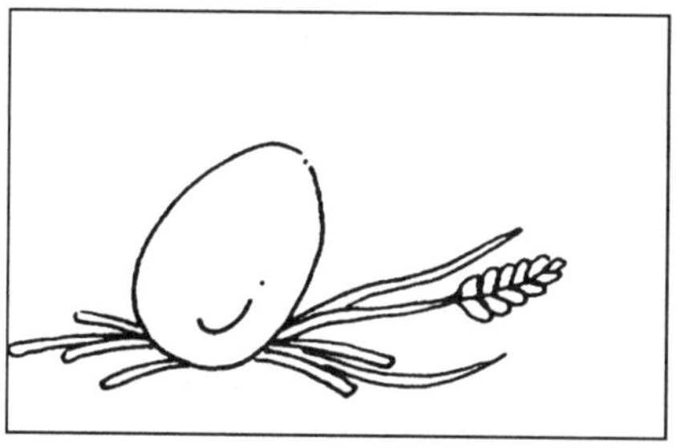 + 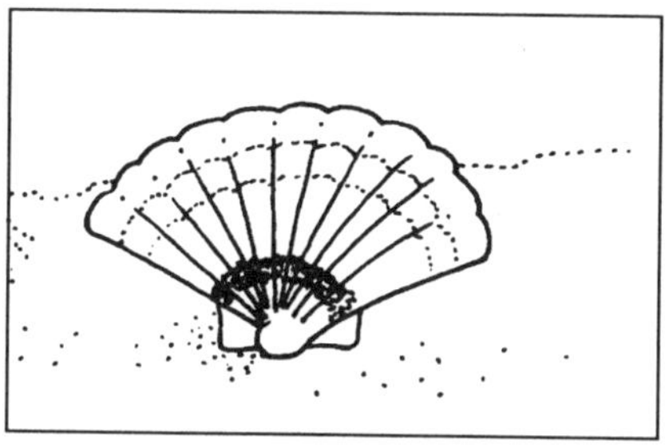 ____________________

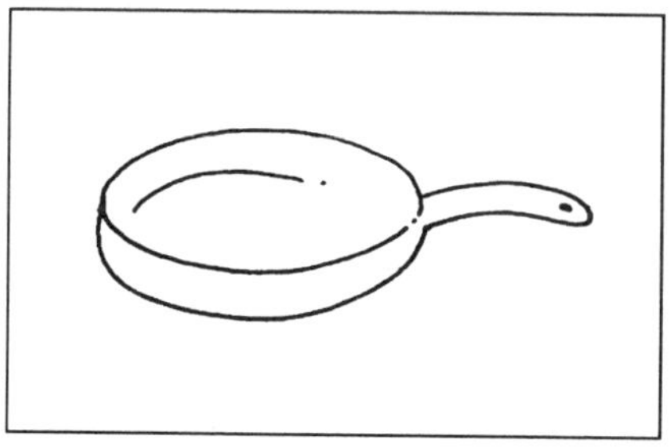 +  ____________________

 + 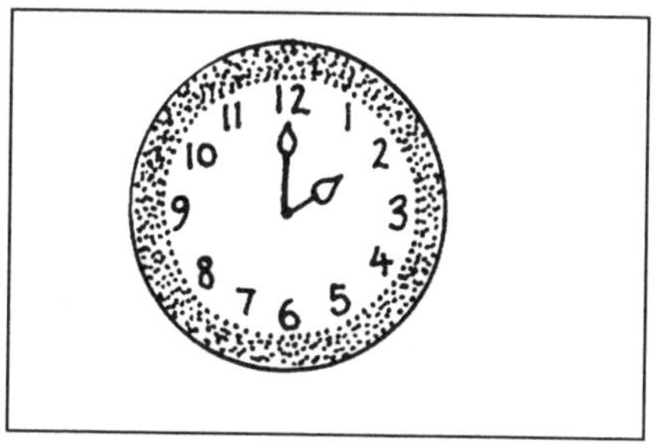

____

▲ Can you think of any other words like these? Write some on the back of this page.

Games and puzzles

Name ____________________

Match the words

Compound words are made up of other words, for example:
rainbow = rain + bow
sunshine = sun + shine

▲ Match a word from each side to work out the compound words about Easter. One has been done for you.

Pass	key
tomb	time
Sun	doing
pan	over
spring	stone
egg	stairs
don	told
wrong	well
fare	shell
up	day
fore	cakes

▲ Can you think of some other compound words? Write them on the back of this page. They do not have to be about Easter. Use a dictionary to help you.

Games and puzzles

Name ____________________

Match the words

Compound words are made up of other words, for example: rainbow = rain + bow sunshine = sun + shine

▲ Match a word from the box below to each word in the list to make some compound words about Easter.

	stone	time	key	shell	told
well		over	cakes	yard	stairs
stand		doing	day		rise

spring____________	pan_____________
sun______________	wrong___________
Pass_____________	fare_____________
egg______________	fore_____________
Sun______________	tomb____________
up_______________	don_____________
under____________	court____________

▲ Now use a dictionary to write down definitions for these words from the list.

don ____

fore____

tomb____

fare____

court____

▲ Use a dictionary to find some more compound words. Write them on the back of this page. The words do not have to be about Easter.

Games and puzzles

Name ______________________

Easter crossword

Across

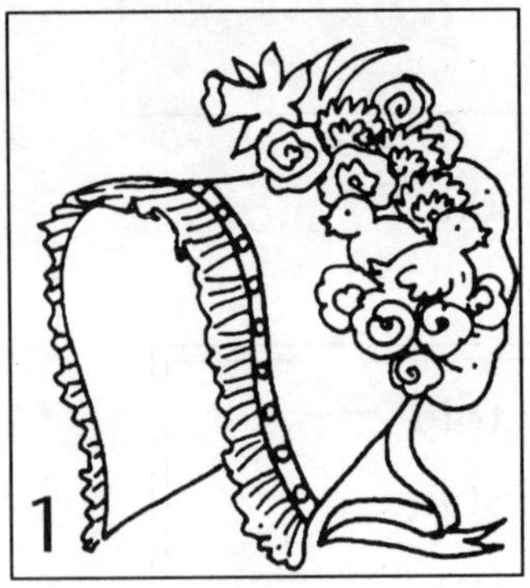
1

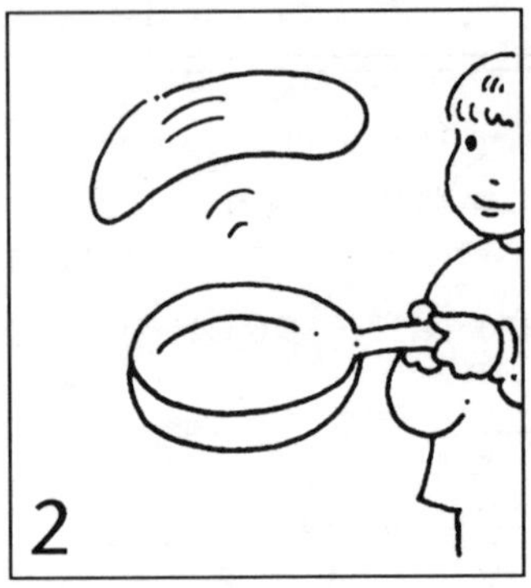
2

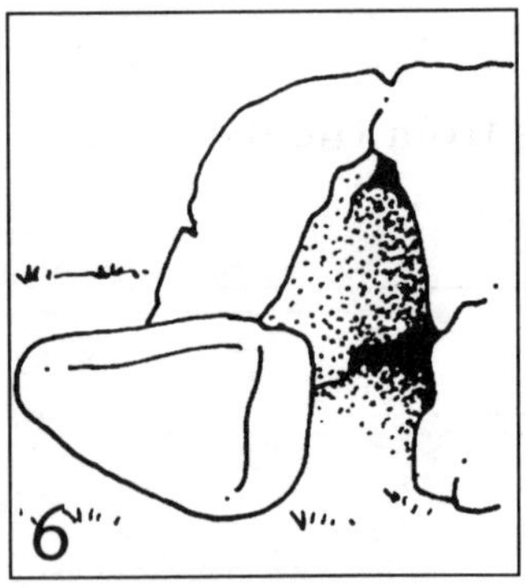
6

7

Jesus bonnet

grave cake

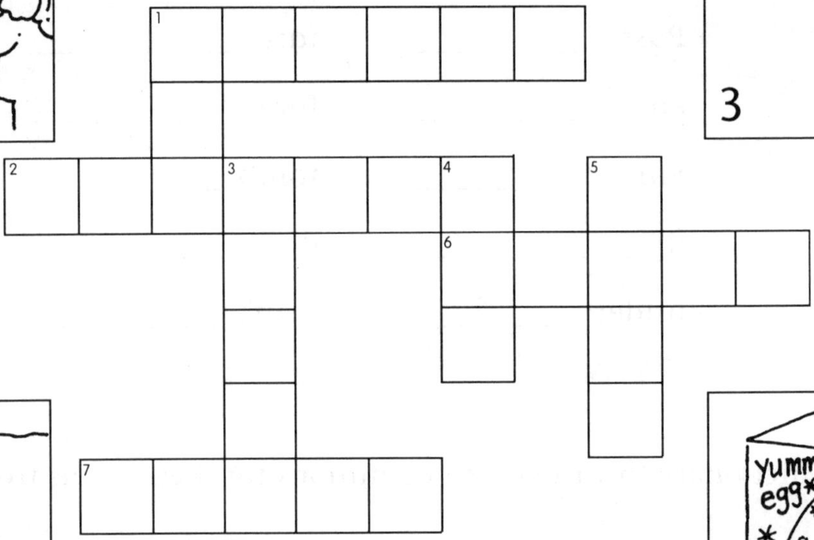

egg cross

pancake

bun

Down

1

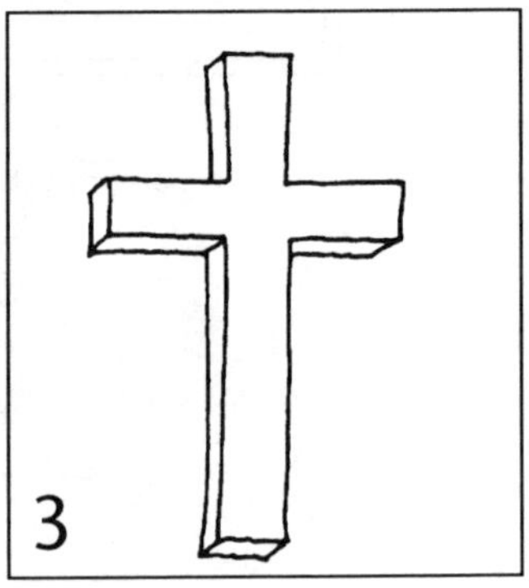
3

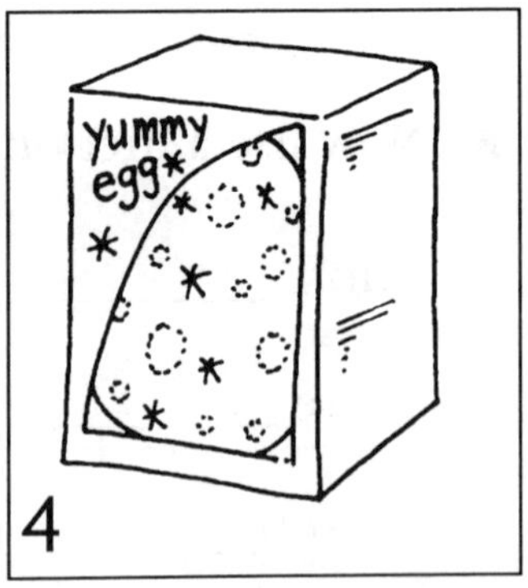
4

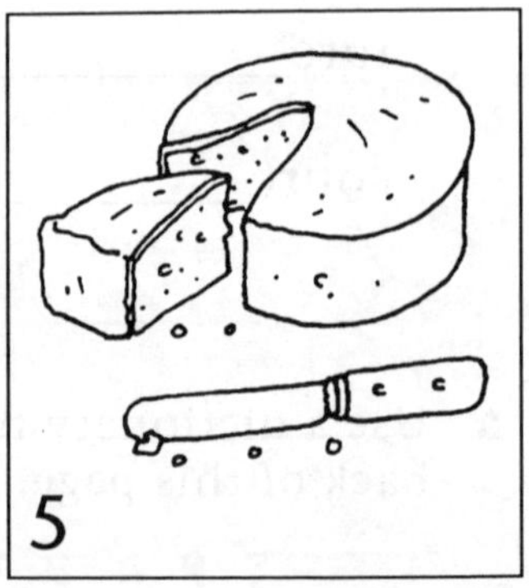
5

Games and puzzles

Name ____________________

Easter crossword

▲ Use the clues below to complete the crossword puzzle.

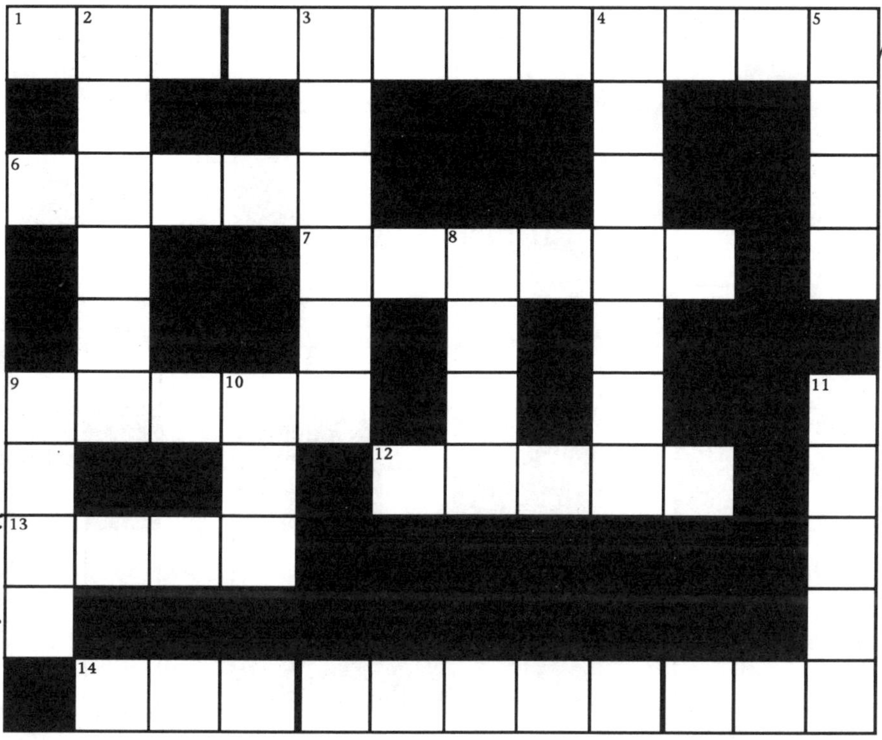

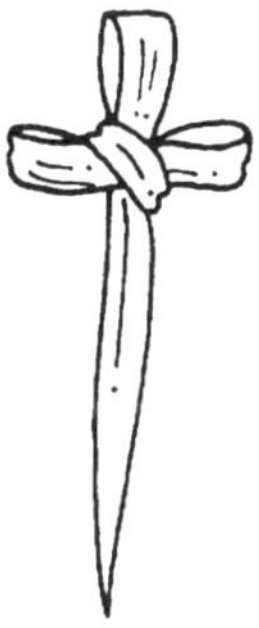

Across

1. The first day of Lent (two words).
6. Jesus died on this.
7. The number of Jesus' disciples.
9. The disciple who said three times that he did not know Jesus.
12. Used to mark people's foreheads with a cross in some churches on Ash Wednesday.
13. The forty days before Easter.
14. A food eaten on Good Friday (three words).

Down

2. Pancake Day = _ _ _ _ _ _ Tuesday.
3. _ _ _ _ _ _ Day is always on a Sunday.
4. The name given to a religious ceremony in church.
5. Easter happens once every _ _ _ _ .
8. People give these at Easter.
9. _ _ _ _ Sunday is the Sunday before Easter.
10. To take in food and swallow it.
11. Jesus was wrapped in this before he was put in the tomb.

Games and puzzles

Name ______________________

Easter crossword

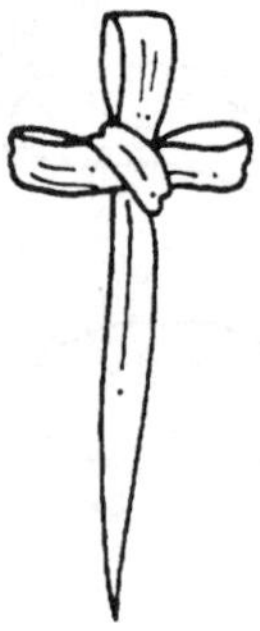

Across

1. The name given to a group of worshippers in church.
5. An eight-day Jewish festival that celebrates the freeing of the Israelites in Egypt.
7. Chocolate confectionary given at Easter.
8. Jesus washed the _ _ _ _ of his disciples before the Passover meal.
9. The disciple who betrayed Jesus.
11. The parade and festival that takes place in some countries on Shrove Tuesday. (2 words)
13. A special cake baked at Easter.
15. To hand over a friend to the enemy.
16. Jesus said that Peter would _ _ _ _ that he knew him three times.
17. Another name for a grave.
18. This was rolled in front of the entrance to Jesus' grave.

Down

1. To put to death by nailing a person to a cross.
2. On Easter Sunday Christians remember how Jesus had _ _ _ _ _ from the dead.
3. The name of the day when Jesus was crucified.
4. The person Christians remember at Easter.
5. The disciple who denied three times to have known Jesus.
6. To be brought back to life from death.
10. This word is an old word that means to be forgiven. Shrove Tuesday is named after this word.
11. Specially minted money given out by the British sovereign on the Thursday before Easter.
12. _ _ _ _ Sunday is the Sunday before Easter.
14. The meal Jesus had with his disciples before he died is called the _ _ _ _ Supper.

Games and puzzles

Name ____________________

Egg puzzle

▲ Join the broken eggs by matching words that sound the same. One has been done for you.

son	poor
wood	hole
wrap	sun
flour	stairs
buy	heal
peel	rap
pour	flower
heel	would
stares	by
whole	peal

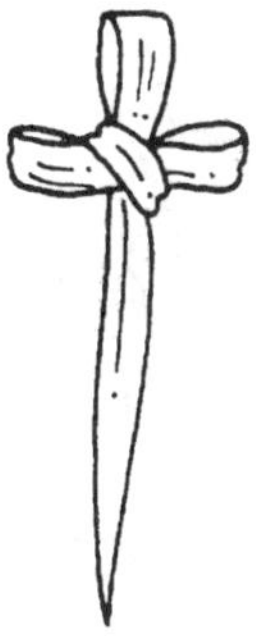

Name ______________________

Egg puzzle

Homophones are words that sound the same but have different meanings and spellings, for example: two and too.

▲ Match the broken eggs by writing the correct homophone in each one. Use a dictionary to help you spell the words. The first one has been done for you.

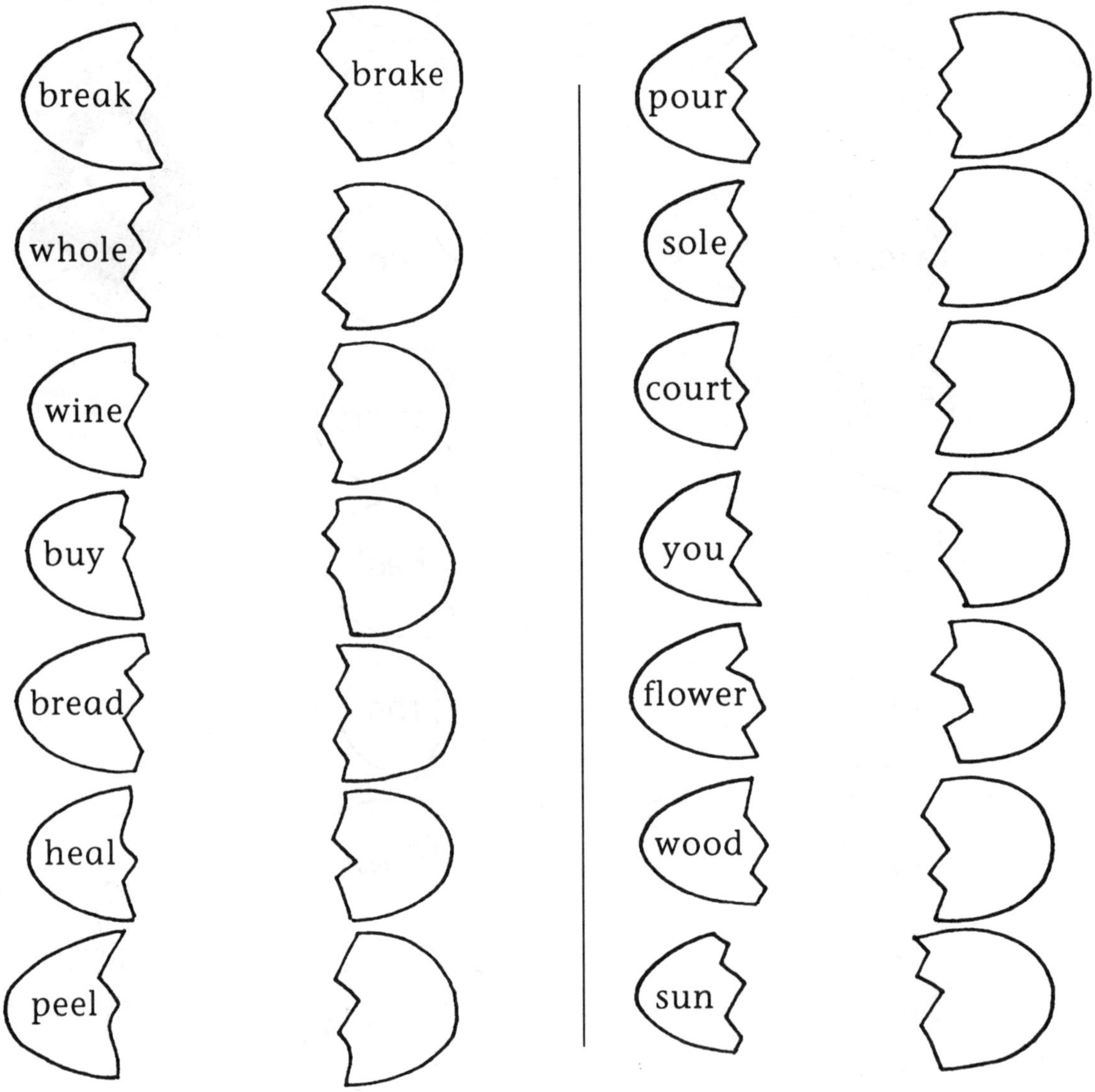

▲ Now write some sentences about Easter using these words.

bread ____

whole ____

peel ____

wine ____

Games and puzzles

Name ______________________

Egg puzzle

Homophones are words that sound the same but have different meanings and spellings, for example: two and too.

▲ Match the broken eggs by writing the correct homophone for each one. Then use a dictionary to write a definition for each word.

Match the eggs	Write a definition for each word in an egg

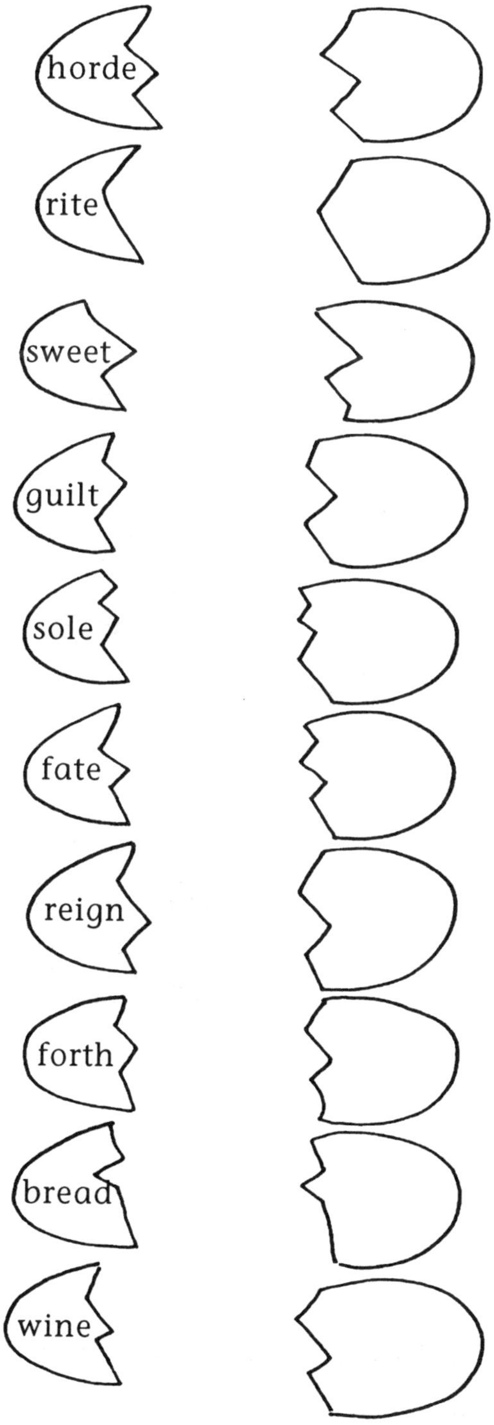

Games and puzzles

Name ____________________

Easter food

Many words have little words inside them. Look at these words:

mother has moth and the in it

card has car in it

▲ Look at these words. Underneath each one write down any little words you can find in it.

pancake bread cream

wine herbs lamb

meat soup flour

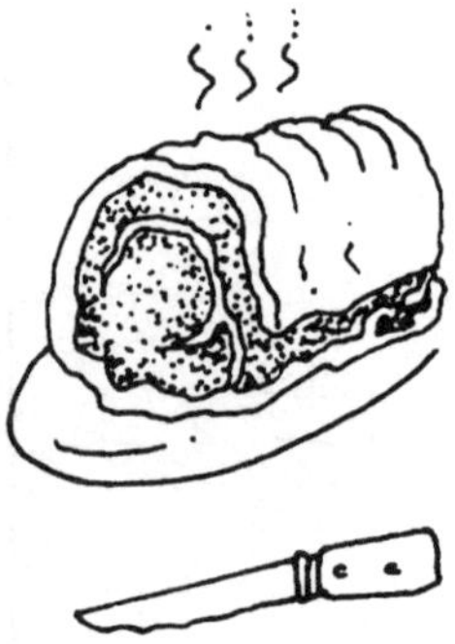

batter chicken cutlets

▲ Now see how many words you can make from the letters in the words hot cross buns. This time you can mix up the order of the letters in the words. For example, you could make sun or not.

Games and puzzles

Name ____________________

Easter food

Many words have little words inside them. Look at these words:

Lenten has Lent and ten in it

Sunday has sun and day in it

▲ Look at these words. Underneath each one write down any little words you can find in it. You must write down at least two little words for each word. Use a dictionary to help you.

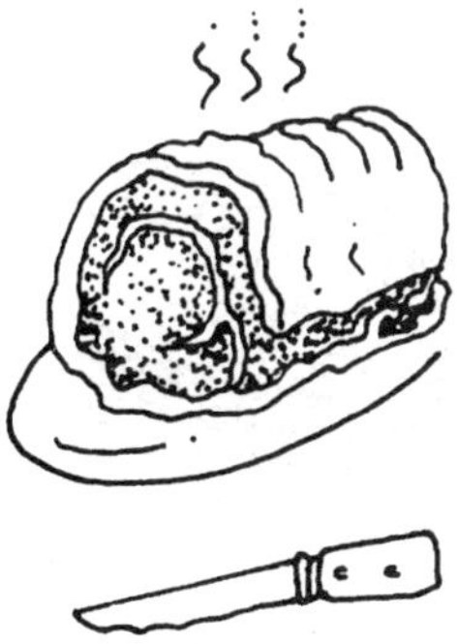

pancake	chocolate	cutlets
mushroom	butter	nutmeg
batter	chicken	meat
cream	almond	margarine

▲ Now see how many words you can make from the letters in the words **simnel cakes**. This time you can mix up the order of the letters in the words. For example, you could make sake or sin. Use a dictionary to help you.

Name ______________________

Easter food

Many words have little words inside them. Look at these words:

Passover has pa, pass, a, as, ass, so and over in it

Donkey has do, don, on and key in it

▲ Look at these words. Underneath each one write down any little words you can find in it. You must write down at least three little words for each word. Use a dictionary to help you.

pancake	chocolate	cutlets
rabbit	marzipan	vegetable
butter	cornflour	potatoes
self-raising flour	watercress	beetroot

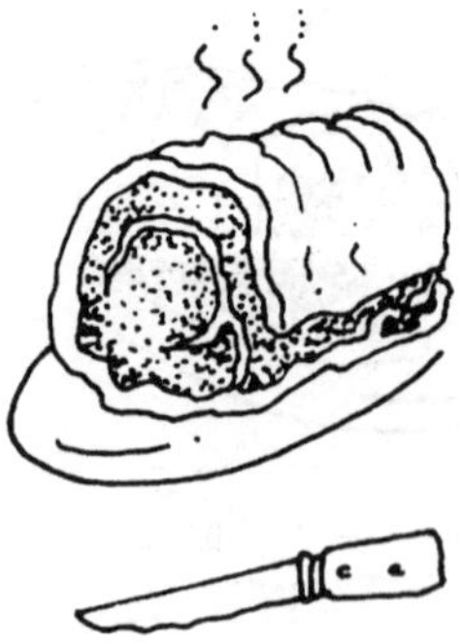

▲ Now see how many words you can make from the letters in the words **unleavened bread**. This time you can mix up the order of the letters in the words. For example, you could make need or under. Use a dictionary to help you.

Stories and poems

Name ________________________

The egg competition

▲ Read this story about Tom.

Tom was very happy today. He couldn't wait to get to school because it was the day of the Easter egg competition. He knew his egg would win because he had spent all last night painting it and he thought it looked really good.

At school Tom looked at the other eggs. He made fun of Emma's egg and made her cry. He held up his egg and told everyone that he was going to win.

Later that day everyone went into the hall to look at the eggs. Mrs Hammond held up the prize. Tom was just about to stand up to get the prize when Mrs Hammond said that Andrew had won. Tom could not understand it. He was very angry and he did not clap with all the others. He did not feel happy for Andrew. All he wanted to do was cry.

▲ Now answer these questions.

What do you think of how Tom behaved? ________________________

____

Write a sentence from the story to show how Tom behaved towards others. ________________________

____

How did Tom feel when he did not win? ________________________

____

Stories and poems

Name ____________________

The egg competition

▲ Read this story then answer the questions.

Today was the day Tom had been waiting for! It was the day of the Easter egg competition at school and Tom had spent many hours last night painting and decorating his egg. He had put so much effort into it that he was sure that he was going to win first prize.

He raced off to school and proudly showed his egg to all his friends. He looked at all the other eggs on display but could not say anything good about them. In fact, he laughed at Emma's egg and made her cry. He then held up his own egg and boasted that he was going to win.

Later that day, everyone was gathered in the hall to hear the winner's name announced. Mrs Hammond was holding up the special first prize and Tom was so sure that he was going to win it that he almost stood up before Mrs Hammond had finished her sentence. But it was Andrew who had won, not Tom. Tom folded his arms in anger and did not clap with everyone else. He was not pleased for Andrew. He simply sat there, staring ahead, with tears burning in his eyes.

What do you think of Tom's behaviour that day? ____________________

____

Which parts of the story show that Tom did not behave kindly towards others? Underline them.

What did Tom do when he did not win? Why do you think he behaved like this? ____________________

____

____

____

Stories and poems

Name ______________________

The egg competition

▲ Read this story then answer the questions.

Tom couldn't contain his excitement. Today was the day of the Easter egg competition at school and he felt absolutely sure that he was going to win because he had spent so much time and effort in creating an elaborate design.

He arrived at school early, determined to make sure everyone knew how spectacular his egg really was! He eagerly viewed all the others on display but did not make any encouraging remarks to anyone. In fact, he sneered and laughed at Emma's egg and ended up making her cry. He even held his egg up and boasted loudly that his was going to be the winner.

It was a very confident Tom, therefore, who entered the school hall later that day to await the announcement of the winner. Mrs Hammond was full of praise for everyone who had entered the competition and she proudly held up the magnificent first prize. Tom was so convinced that the prize would be his, that he almost stood up before Mrs Hammond had even finished speaking! He was stunned, therefore, when he realised that he had not won at all, and that Andrew was making his way to the front of the hall. Everyone clapped and cheered loudly as Andrew received his prize. Everyone, that is, except for Tom who merely sat there with his arms folded tightly, fuming silently with angry tears threatening to fall.

What is your opinion about Tom's behaviour that morning? Why do you think he was so confident? ______________________

____

____

Which one sentence from the story shows that Tom behaved unkindly towards others? Write the sentence here. ______________________

____

How do you think Tom should have behaved instead? ______________________

____

____

▲ On the back of this sheet, write down how Tom behaved when he did not win. What do you think of his behaviour? Support your ideas by referring to the story.

Name ______________________

The pancake race

▲ Look at this comic strip. Finish the story. Write something in a speech bubble in your story.

Stories and poems

Name ___________________

The pancake race

▲ Complete the comic strip by writing what you think each person is saying. Draw and write a suitable ending in the last box. Use the words below to help you.

enter	pancake	race	beat	hope	win	knew
winning	run	fast	slow	look	going	

Stories and poems

Name ____________________

The pancake race

▲ Complete the comic strip by writing what you think each person is saying. Draw and write suitable ideas in each blank frame so that the story makes sense.

Stories and poems

Name ______________________

The Easter holidays

▲ Read this story about Tanya's Easter holiday.

Tanya was very happy. She was going to spend the Easter holidays with her aunty in France. When she got to the airport with her parents, they found out that the plane trip was going to be ten hours late! Tanya was very upset.

They went to a hotel. The food wasn't very good and the room was cold. Next day, they went on the plane to France. The trip was good but they could not find their cases at the airport. They had gone missing!

Tanya and her parents had to wear the same clothes every day until their cases were found. Tanya wished that she had stayed home instead!

▲ Now write about an Easter holiday you have had. Say why it was good or bad.

____

____

____

____

____

____

____

____

Name ______________________

The Easter holiday

▲ Read this story about Tanya's Easter holiday.

Tanya was very excited about Easter this year as she was going on her first trip to France to stay with her aunty there. She packed her suitcase and couldn't wait to get to the airport. But when she arrived there with her parents, they were told that the plane was going to be delayed for ten hours!

Tanya was very upset but she tried to cheer herself up by thinking about the hotel they were going to stay in overnight. But it was a disaster! The food was terrible and the rooms were freezing cold.

Tanya and her parents arrived at the airport the next day in a bad mood, thinking that something else might go wrong, but the flight was terrific. Unfortunately, luck was not to remain on their side, because their suitcases went missing and they were forced to spend several days in the same clothes until the cases were found.

Tanya loved seeing her aunty, but she wished she had stayed at home instead!

▲ Now write about an Easter holiday you have had. Explain why it was a good or bad holiday.

____

____

____

____

____

____

____

____

Stories and poems

Name ______________________

The Easter holiday

▲ Read this story about Tanya's Easter holiday.

Tanya had been looking forward to the Easter holidays for some time because it was going to be her first time abroad. She and her parents were going to stay with her aunty in France. She was so excited about the trip that on the day of departure she was ready three hours too early for the coach trip to the airport!

On arrival they were informed that their flight was going to be delayed for ten hours. Tanya and her parents were very annoyed and disappointed, but they decided to make the most of it by enjoying their stay at the hotel they were booked into overnight. But unfortunately that was a disaster too because the food was appalling and the room was freezing! Understandably, they arrived at the airport in a foul mood the next day and were anticipating further trouble.

The flight, however, was excellent and Tanya really enjoyed her first plane trip. They hoped the holiday would now run smoothly, but their luggage could not be found at the other end and they had to endure wearing the same clothes for many days until their cases were found. Tanya enjoyed seeing France and staying with her aunty but she wished that she had stayed home as usual instead!

▲ Now write about an Easter holiday you have experienced.
Say why you enjoyed it or not.

____

____

____

____

____

____

____

____

Name ____________________

The great egg robbery

▲ Complete this story. Use the pictures and the words in the box to help you.

One day, Hetty and Penny were looking at ____________________ ____________ in the shop window. They thought the eggs looked ____________________ . Just as Hetty and Penny were leaving, some men came in a van. Hetty and Penny hid behind the shop. The men ____ .
Hetty and Penny ran to their friends. They got all their eggs and ran to the road. They ____________________________ ____ .
The van fell over and the ____________________________ ____ .
Hetty and Penny had helped to catch the robbers!

Easter	chocolate	lovely	nice	better
broke	window	threw	lots	going
policemen	stopped	caught		

Name ______________________

The great egg robbery

▲ Draw a picture in the last box to complete this story. Then write the whole story in your own words. Use a dictionary to help you.

____

____

____

____

____

____

____

____

____

____

____

Continue on the back of this sheet.

Name ____________________

The great egg robbery

▲ Look at the pictures below. They show the beginning of a story. Decide what might happen next and then write the whole story. Use a dictionary to help you.

▲ Include the following things in your story:

1 An interesting beginning, explaining who the hens are and why they are looking at the shop display
2 Who the robbers are and why they are stealing the eggs
3 What the hens decide to do to catch the robbers
4 An exciting ending, explaining what happens to the robbers

____

____

____

____

____

____

____

____

____

____

____

____

____

____

Continue on the back of this sheet.

Stories and poems

Name ____________________

Easter delights!

▲ *Read this poem about making a pancake.*

Pancake Mix

Stir the mixture,
Whish, bang, whish, bang.
Pour it in a pan,
Slush, slop, slush, slop.
Watch it cook,
Hiss, bubble, hiss, bubble.
Eat it quick!
Munch, crunch, munch, crunch!

▲ *The poem has a lot of sound words in it like 'whish', 'slop' and 'hiss' that help us to 'hear' the sounds made when making a pancake.*

▲ *Add some sound words to this poem about Easter eggs. Decorate the poem.*

Easter Eggs

Feel the wrapper,
____________________,
Tear the paper,
____________________,
Smell the chocolate,
____________________,
Eat it up!
____________________.

Name ____________________

Easter delights!

▲ Read this poem about making a pancake. It uses words that sound like their meaning, such as 'plop' and 'hiss'. This helps us to 'hear' the sounds of the things happening in the poem.

Pancake Mix

Sift the salt and flour,
Shake, bang, shake, bang.
Break the egg,
Snap, crack, snap, crack.
Put it in the flour,
Sloop, plop, sloop, plop.
Beat the mixture,
Whisk, whir, whisk, whir.
Put it in a pan,
Slush, slop, slush, slop.
Watch it cook,
Hiss, bubble, hiss, bubble.
Turn it quick,
Swoosh, flip, swoosh, flip.
Eat it quick!
Munch, gobble, munch, gobble!

▲ Add your own sound words to this poem about Easter eggs. You can make up words if you want to. Illustrate your poem.

Easter Eggs

Feel the wrapper,

____________________ .

Shake the egg,

____________________ .

Tear the paper,

____________________ .

Smell the chocolate,

____________________ .

Break the egg,

____________________ .

Eat it up!

____________________ .

▲ Now make up your own sound poem about hot cross buns.

Stories and poems

Name ____________________

Easter delights!

▲ Read this poem about making a pancake. It uses words that sound like their meaning, such as 'plop' and 'hiss'. These words are called onomatopoeia and they help us to 'hear' the sounds of the things happening in the poem.

Pancake Mix

Sift the salt and flour,
Shake, bang, shake, bang.
Break the egg,
Snap, crack, snap, crack.
Put it in the flour,
Sloop, plop, sloop, plop.
Beat the mixture,
Whisk, whir, whisk, whir.
Put it in a pan,
Slush, slop, slush, slop.
Watch it cook,
Hiss, bubble, hiss, bubble.
Turn it quick,
Swoosh, flip, swoosh, flip.
Eat it quick!
Munch, gobble, munch, gobble!

▲ Write your own sound poem like the one above, using onomatopoeic words. You can invent sound words of your own! The first two lines have been done for you.

Easter Eggs

Feel the wrapper,
Crackle, crinkle, crackle, crinkle.

Name ______________________

Springtime

▲ Read this poem about daffodils.

Daffodils

Spring is here at last – I've been waiting for this day
All the flowers are blooming and are here to stay
I can see some daffodils, one, two, three
Oh what a lovely sight they are to see!

▲ The last words in each line rhyme. Circle the words below that also rhyme with day and stay.

May try my bay say by today

▲ Now circle the words below that rhyme with three and see.

me bee make he she been these

▲ Now match these spring words by joining the words that rhyme.

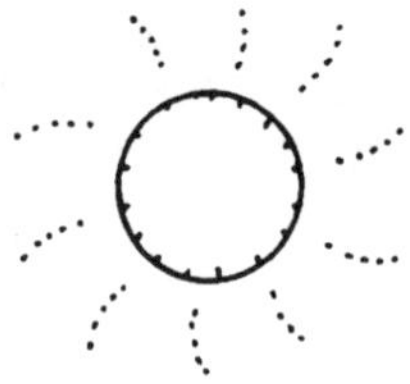

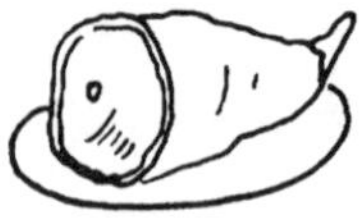

▲ Write your own spring poem using words that rhyme.

Stories and poems

Name ____________________

Springtime

▲ Read this poem about daffodils by A. A. Milne.

Daffodowndilly

She wore her yellow sun-bonnet,
  She wore her greenest gown;
She turned to the south wind
  And curtsied up and down.
She turned to the sunlight
  And shook her yellow head,
And whispered to her neighbour:
  'Winter is dead.'

▲ These words in the poem rhyme: **gown** and **down** **head** and **dead**

▲ Think of some more words that rhyme to add to these two lists:

gown clown brown frown	head red said spread

▲ Now use some of these words to complete the lines below to make a new poem.

Daffodil

She wore her yellow sun-bonnet,
  She ____________________
She turned to the south wind
  And ____________________
She turned to the sunlight
  And ____________________
And whispered to her neighbour:

____

▲ Write your own poem about spring, using words that rhyme.

Name ____________________

Springtime

▲ Read these two verses of a poem about daffodils written by William Wordsworth.

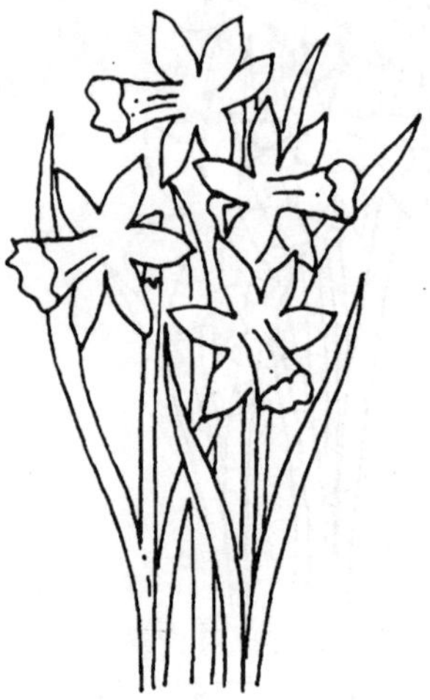

Daffodils

I wander'd lonely as a cloud
That floats on high o'er vales and hills,
When all at once I saw a crowd,
A host of golden daffodils;
Beside the lake, beneath the trees,
Fluttering and dancing in the breeze.

Continuous as the stars that shine
And twinkle on the Milky Way,
They stretch'd in never-ending line
Along the margin of a bay:
Ten thousand saw I at a glance,
Tossing their heads in sprightly dance.

▲ Use a rhyming dictionary to find as many words as you can to compile these lists of rhyming words:

cloud crowd	hills daffodils	trees breeze	shine line	way bay	glance dance
________	________	________	________	________	________
________	________	________	________	________	________
________	________	________	________	________	________
________	________	________	________	________	________
________	________	________	________	________	________

▲ Now use some of these words to write your own rhyming poem about something to do with Spring. You may like to copy the rhyming pattern in William Wordsworth's poem.

Name ______________________

Easter time

▲ *Read these poems about Easter.*

Easter treats

Pancake batter
Chocolate egg
Spicy fruit buns
And roast lamb leg

Easter time

At Easter time
We eat fruit buns
We make pancakes
And have some fun

▲ *These poems use a syllable pattern. Count the syllables for the words in each line of the poem to find out what the pattern is.*

First line = ________ syllables
Second line = ________ syllables
Third line = ________ syllables
Fourth line = ________ syllables

▲ *Use the same syllable pattern to complete this poem about Easter. Use the words in the box to help you.*

Easter time

At Easter time
We ______________________
We ______________________
And ______________________

church	sing	songs
play	games	eat
visit	friends	card
mother	pancake	race
hunt	unwrap	eggs

Stories and poems

Name ______________________

Easter time

▲ Read these poems about Easter.

Easter is the time
When Christians remember how
Jesus died for us

Delicious pancakes
Spicy, tasty hot cross buns
Easter food delights!

▲ Both poems are haikus – a Japanese form of poetry that has 17 syllables, written in three lines, like this:

first line	– 5 syllables
second line	– 7 syllables
third line	– 5 syllables

▲ Complete these haikus about Easter. Make sure you count the syllables!

Easter time is ______________
We eat lots of ______________
And ______________________

Late breakfast __________________
And __________________________
Mothering Sunday

▲ Now write some Easter haikus of your own. Use the word box below for ideas on what to write about.

Lent	Shrove Tuesday
Palm Sunday	Mother's Day
Good Friday	Passover
chocolate eggs	holidays
Mardi Gras	carnival
hot cross buns	simnel cake
pancake races	egg hunt

Stories and poems

Name ______________________

Easter time

▲ Read these poems about Easter.

Easter
A time of death
A time of new life, hope
When Jesus was resurrected
Rejoice!

Easter
Tasty pancakes
Yummy chocolate eggs
Delicious, fruity hot cross buns
Easter

▲ These poems are both cinquains – a type of poem that has 5 lines and 22 syllables. The syllables are set out in the following way:

first line – 2 syllables
second line – 4 syllables
third line – 6 syllables
fourth line – 8 syllables
fifth line – 2 syllables

▲ The short first line often introduces the topic and the last line usually makes a statement or some kind of impact. The lines can run on from each other, for example:

Mother,
I do love you
Even when you get cross
When I am very annoying.
Love you!

▲ Write some Easter time cinquains of your own. The poems could be written about: Shrove Tuesday, Palm Sunday, Easter Day, Lent, Mothering Sunday, Maundy Thursday or Easter foods and customs.

Continue on the back of this sheet.

Name ______________________

Carnival

▲ Read this poem about an Easter carnival.

Carnival

It's carnival day today!
Come join us on the street
We'll be dancing, singing and clapping
And skipping on our feet.

It's carnival day today!
Come join us for a treat
We'll be feasting, running and rolling
And moving to the beat.

▲ This poem uses lots of doing words like 'dancing', 'singing' and 'clapping'. We could make these words look like their meaning, like this:

▲ Now you do the same with these words:

running

rolling

Name ______________________

Carnival

▲ Read the first verse of this poem about an Easter carnival.

Carnival

It's carnival day today!
Come join us on the STREET
We'll be dancing, singing and clapping
And skipping on our feet

▲ This poem is a calligram, where some of the words in the poem are made to look like their meaning. The second verse of the poem is written below. Make it into a calligram by re-writing the poem, making some of the words look like their meaning.

It's carnival day today!
Come join us for a treat
We'll be feasting, running and rolling
And moving to the beat.

Stories and poems

Name ____________________

Carnival

▲ Read this poem about an Easter carnival.

Carnival

It's carnival day today!
Come join us on the street
We'll be dancing, singing and clapping
And skipping on our feet.

It's carnival day today!
Come join us for a treat
We'll be feasting, running and rolling
And moving to the beat.

▲ Re-write the poem as a calligram by making some of the words look like their meaning, for example, the line: 'Come join us on the street' could look like this:

Come *join* us on the STREET

Name ____________________

An Easter card

▲ Colour in the front of the card. Draw and colour a picture on the back page. Write your name and the date. Cut out the card along the dotted lines. Fold the card in half. Write a message inside.

Happy Easter

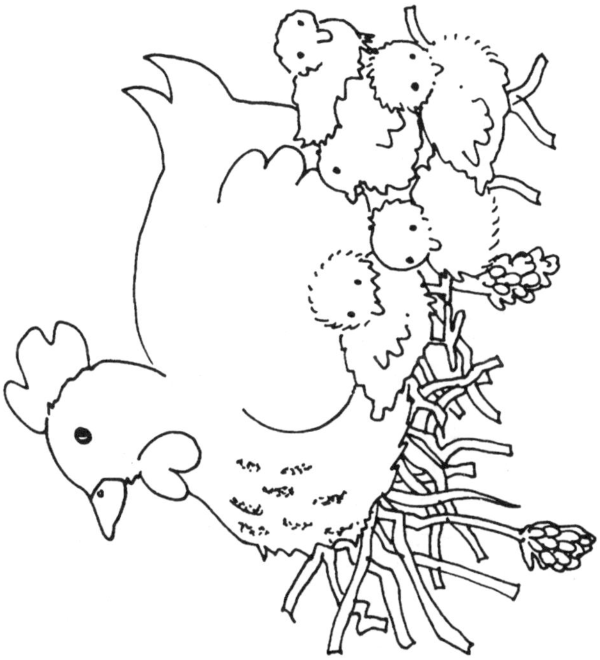

This card was made by ____________________

Date: ____________________

Name ____________________

An Easter card

1 Cut out and glue small pieces of coloured paper or foil onto the rabbit outline to make an interesting pattern.
2 Draw and colour a design on the back page. Write your name and date.
3 Cut along the dotted lines. Fold the card in half. Write a message inside.

Happy Easter

This card was made by: ____________________

Date: ____________________

Things to do

Name ______________________

An Easter card

▲ Follow these instructions to make this card:

1. Draw and colour some designs on the large Easter egg and ribbon.
2. Draw and colour designs on each small egg. Colour the rest of the card.
3. Cut around the outside of the card. Carefully cut around the top part of the egg.
4. Fold back the card at 'a' so that the egg stands up.
5. Glue some paper over the cut-out section.
6. Fill in your name in the space provided.
7. Write a message inside the card.

Things to do

Name ______________________

Easter egg designs

▲ Finish each egg by continuing the pattern. Colour them in.

1

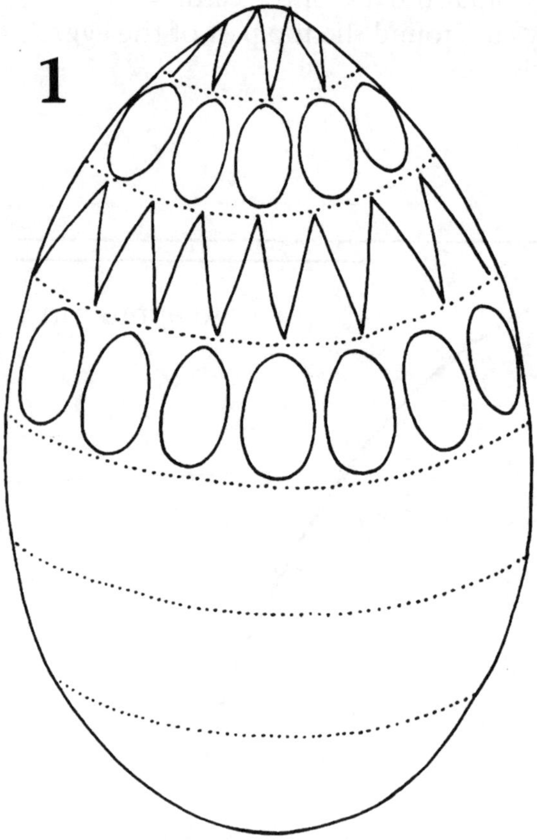

2

▲ Which design do you like best? 1 or 2? ________

▲ Write down why you like this one best.

____

____

▲ Complete this advertising jingle to sell this egg.

Buy ______________ eggs
They really are the best
They're __________ and ______________
And ______________ the rest!

Name ______________________

Easter egg designs

▲ Draw a different design on each egg. Colour them in using only four colours.

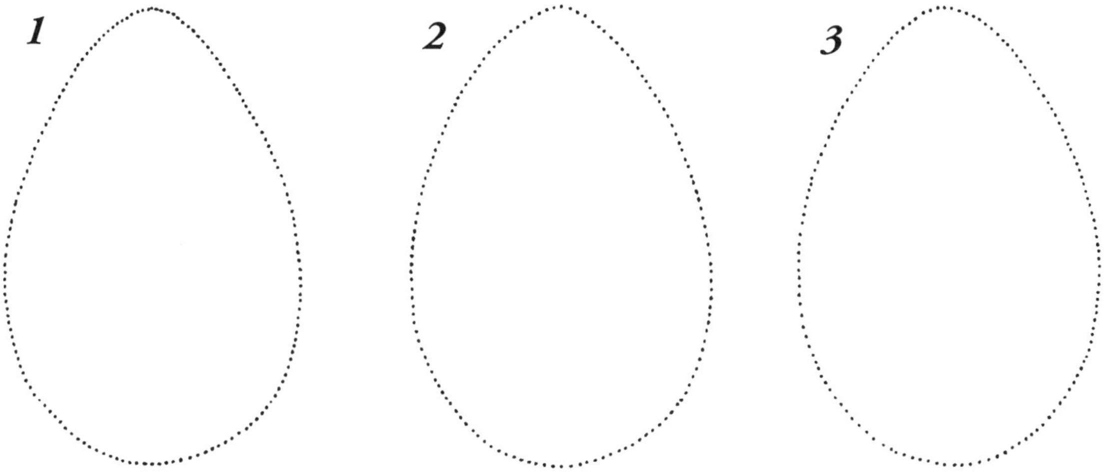

▲ Write down which egg design you prefer, giving your reasons why.

____

____

____

▲ Now design an advertisement to sell this egg. Invent a name for the egg. Tell people why they should buy it. Include the price. Complete the jingle.

New this Easter!

Buy ______________________
You really won't regret it
They're ______________________
____

Things to do

Name ______________________

Easter egg designs

▲ Use this design brief to design an Easter egg and a poster to advertise it. Make sure you include everything the customer wants!

Design brief

Our company would like you to design an Easter egg and advertisement with all the following things:

1 Interesting, colourful egg design that includes a chicken.
2 A colourful poster with the egg's name written very large.
3 Five reasons why people should buy the egg to be on the poster.
4 A catchy, 4-line jingle that rhymes to be included on the poster.
5 The price to be shown clearly.

▲ Draw your egg design here.

▲ Draw your poster here.

▲ On the back of this page, evaluate your egg and poster. What things are good? What things could be improved?

Things to do

Name ______________________

Easter cooking

▲ Complete these instructions for making pancakes by using the words and pictures to help you. Then, with adult help, cook some pancakes of your own!

1

You will need:
1 cup of flour
1egg
1/4 teaspoon salt
1 1/4 cups of milk
1 tablespoon butter
2 tablespoons caster sugar
juice of 1 lemon

2

3

4

1 Collect and weigh the ingredients.

2 Sift flour and ______________ .

3 Add the __________ and a little__________. Beat well for 1 minute.

4 Add rest of __________. Mix until __________.

5 Melt ______________ in frying pan.

6 Pour in some batter. __________ until set and lightly brown.

7 Turn or toss the ______________ . Cook other side.

8 Remove from pan. Sprinkle with ______________ and ______________ . Serve at once.

5

6

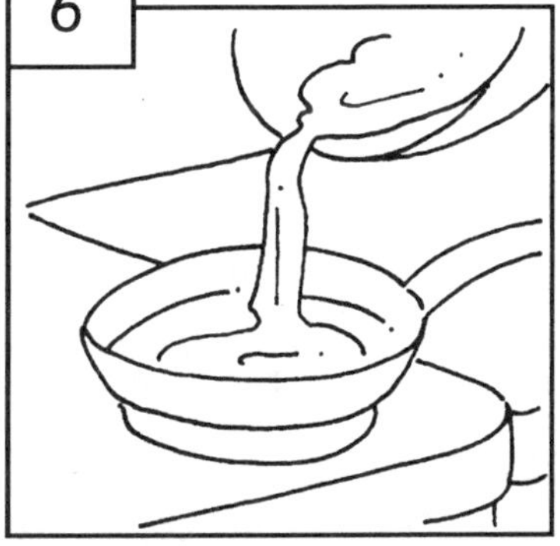

7

8

Things to do

Name ______________________

Easter cooking

▲ Complete the instructions for this recipe to make a simnel cake by using the diagrams to help you. Then make the cake with adult help.

Cake:		**Almond paste:**
3 tablespoons butter	120g sultanas	240g almond meal
3/4 cup sugar	120g currants	460g caster sugar
2 cups flour	120g raisins	2 beaten eggs
1 teaspoon baking powder	60g chopped mixed peel	1 teaspoon vanilla
4 eggs	1/2 teaspoon grated nutmeg	

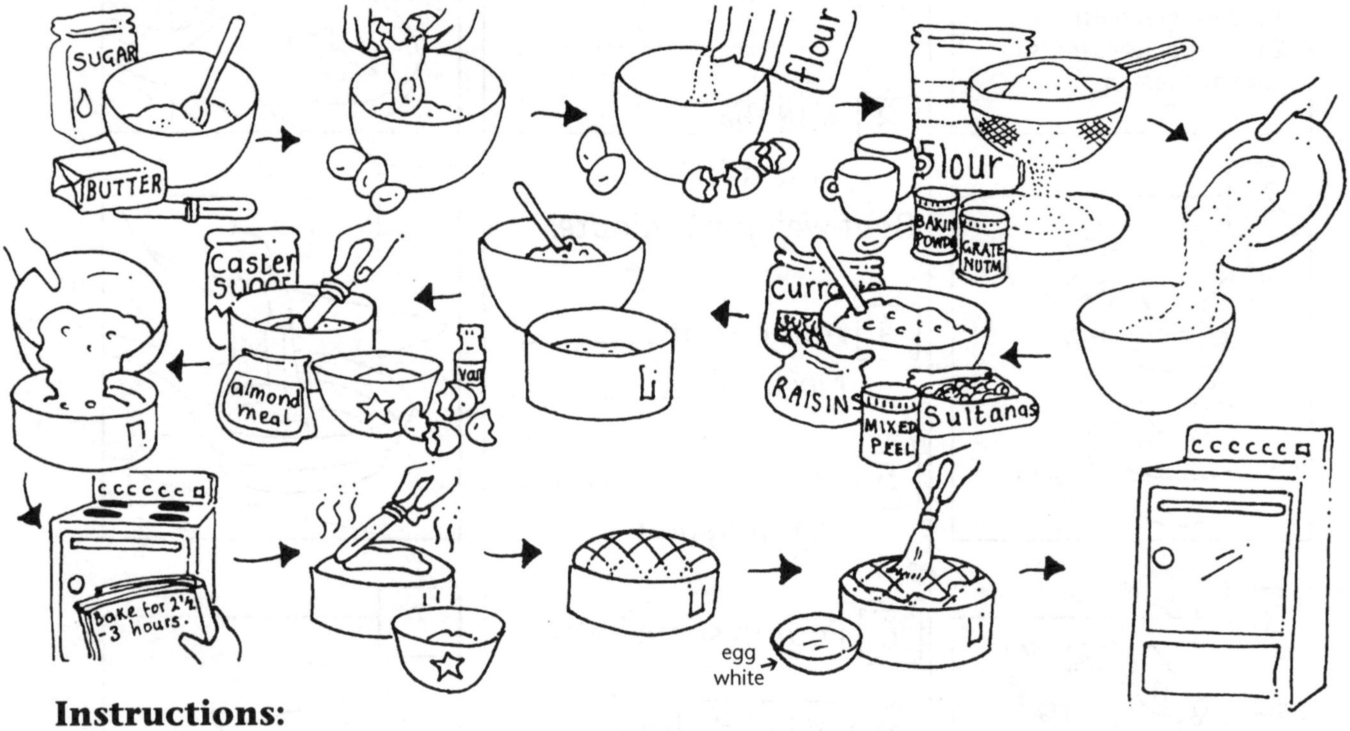

Instructions:

Cream the ________ and ________ until light and fluffy. ______________, one at a time. Add a small amount of flour after the first two eggs are in. Sift the rest of the __________, together with the ____________________ and __________. Add this to the ____________. Stir in the ___________ ____________________________ and mixed peel. Put half the mixture into a greased cake tin.

Mix the ____________ to make the almond paste and spread half of this over the cake mix in the tin. Then ______________________________.

Bake in a moderate oven for _________________. When the cake is nearly cooked, take it out of the ________ and spread the rest of __________ ___________________. Mark the top in squares or diamonds. Brush the top of the cake with a little ____________. Put back in oven until cooked.

Things to do

Name ______________________

Easter cooking

▲ On another piece of paper, write the instructions for this recipe to make hot cross buns. Use the information and diagrams below to help you. Then make the buns with adult supervision.

Ingredients:

460g plain flour	1 egg	60g butter	150ml warm water
30g yeast	60g sugar	60g sultanas	150ml milk

Note

To glaze the buns, mix 1 tablespoon sugar, 1 teaspoon of cinnamon and 1 tablespoon of hot water. Put on the top of the cooked buns and return to the oven for a few minutes.

Name ____________________

Easter bonnet parade

▲ Use the pictures and words below to complete the sentences.

bonnet

rabbits

eggs

chickens

daffodils

prize

This is a picture of Julia. She is in the Easter ______________ Parade.

She is wearing a lovely bonnet. The bonnet has r __________ , e__________ and c ____________ on it.

On the rim of the bonnet are lots of ______________________ .

Julia won first __________ in the parade for having the best bonnet.

Things to do

Name ____________________

Easter bonnet parade

▲ Look at this picture of a person in an Easter bonnet parade. Choose words from the box to write a report.

word box

bonnet	card
daffodils	better
rabbits	father
Monday	paper
planning	eggs
pleased	Easter
parade	prize

On __________ all the children in Wellbeck School took part in an Easter Bonnet ____________. Julia Young won first _________ for her wonderful ____________. It had chickens, ___________ and Easter ______ all over it. It also had lots of yellow ____________ around the rim.

The bonnet is made of coloured _______ and all the decorations are made of ______. Julia's __________ made the bonnet and he was very ____________ that Julia won. He is already ___________ a bonnet for next year's __________ parade which he thinks will be even _______ than this one!

Things to do

Name ______________________

Easter bonnet parade

▲ Write a report for a school magazine about this picture of Julia Young. She won first prize in an Easter bonnet parade at Wellbeck School. Describe the bonnet in detail and how you think Julia might feel. Use words from the box and a dictionary to help you. Make your report interesting to read.

magnificent	exciting
decorated	procession
elaborate	design
daffodils	chickens
cellophane	coloured
wonderful	creation
judges	decided
extremely	pleased
display	certificate

▲ Write your report here.

Continue on the back of this sheet.

Things to do

Name ______________________

Spring flowers

▲ *This flower is a daffodil. Label the parts of the daffodil by using the writing in the box to help you. Colour the daffodil in the correct colours.*

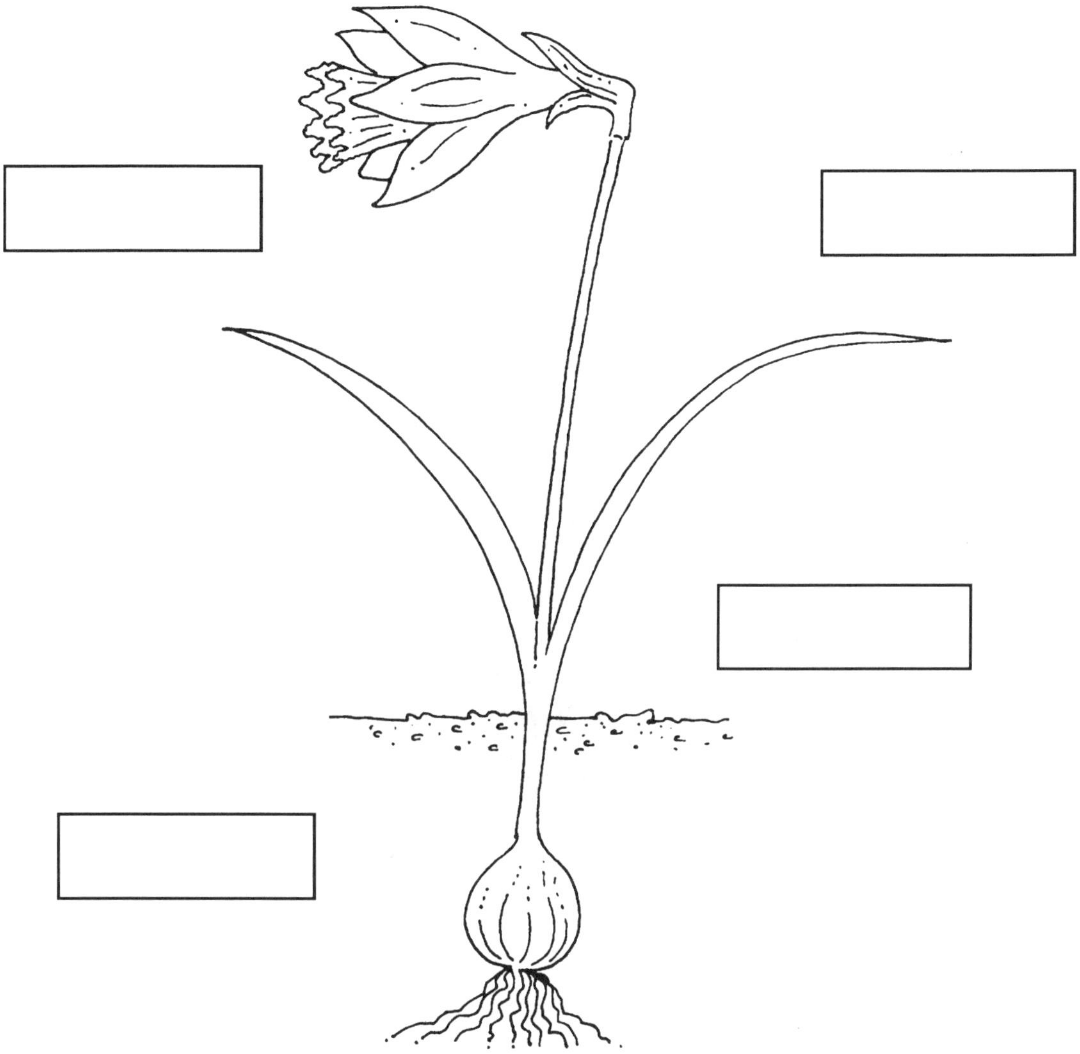

The daffodil flowers in spring. It grows in many places and lots of people grow them in their gardens. The flower at the top of the plant is often very yellow. Below the flower is a long stem. It is very strong and helps to keep the plant up. The stem is green. At the bottom of the stem are some leaves. They are quite long and pointy. The leaves are also green. Under the soil, the plant has roots. The roots suck up water for the daffodil. The roots are grey.

Things to do

Name ____________________

Spring flowers

▲ This flower is a cowslip. Label and colour the diagram correctly, using the information in the box to help you.

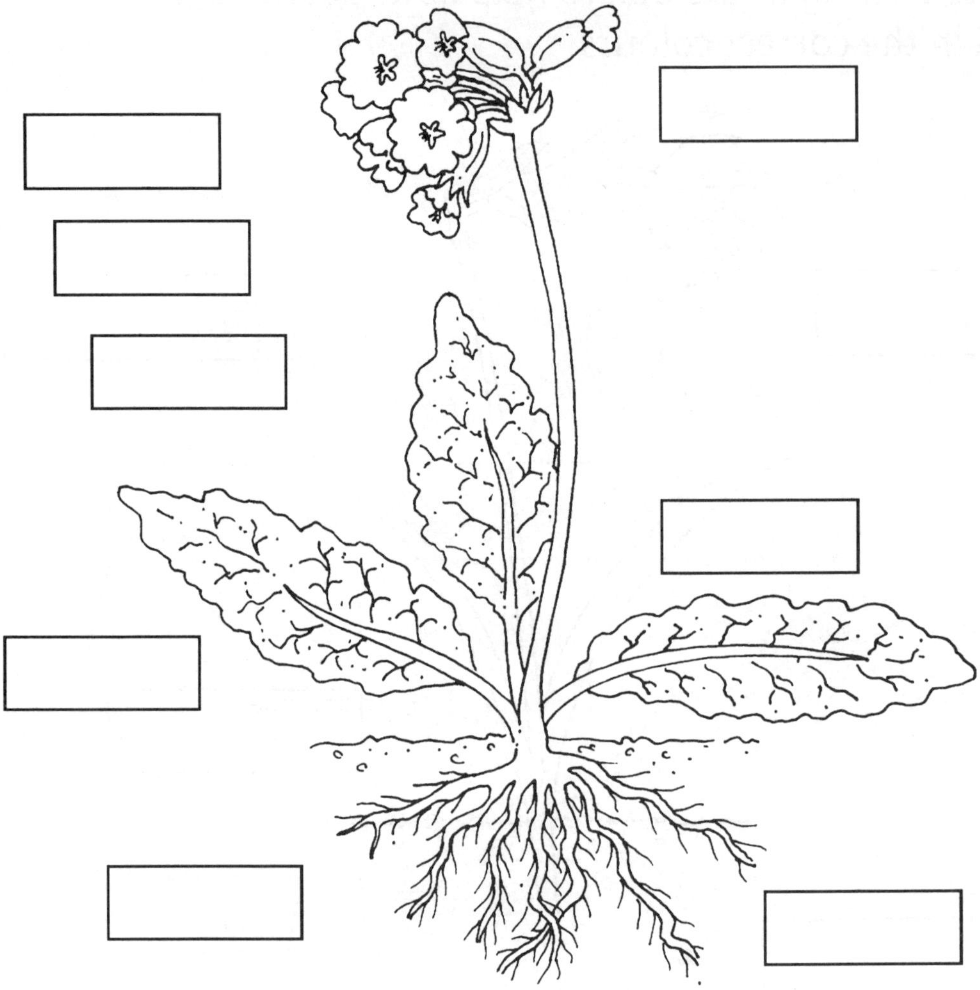

The cowslip is a spring wild flower that grows in grassy places, often on hillsides and motorway verges. It is found throughout Britain but is rare in Scotland. It has large wrinkled dark-green leaves that form a ground rosette. In the centre of this rosette is a long light-green stem without leaves. At the top of the stem is a cluster of yellow flowers. The bright yellow petals are joined together to form a tube that is partly covered up by the green sepals that also form a tube. Short orange-coloured stamens are in the centre of each flower. At the base of the stem, underneath the soil are the grey-white roots that are quite thick. Fine root hairs grow along each root. The flowers can be used to make cowslip wine.

Things to do

Name ______________________

Spring flowers

▲ This flower is called Goldilocks. Label and colour the diagram correctly by using the information provided.

Goldilocks (*Ranunculus auricomus)* is a spring-flowering wild flower found throughout much of Britain. The plant flowers during April and May and grows to a height of 15–45cm. There are only a few flowers on each plant. The flowers are golden-yellow with five stunted petals although some flowers have no petals at all. In from the petals are many pollen-covered orange stamens forming an inner ring around the numerous central carpels. Inside the carpels are the ovules that contain the eggs of the plant. After pollination, these carpels ripen and form hairy fruits with a single seed inside. The plant has several long spindly light-green stems that have stalkless leaves on them. These dark-green leaves are palmate (shaped like an open hand). At the base of the stems is another clump of leaves that can vary in size and shape. They are either rounded or kidney-shaped. The whole plant is firmly supported in the ground by the roots that are covered in tiny root hairs. Goldilocks grow in deciduous woodlands, especially in damp mixed and oak woods. They also grow in wet meadows and on rocky ground in hills and mountains.

Things to do

Name ____________________

An Easter game

▲ You are going to make an Easter board game. Complete the rules and game by writing words in the spaces so the sentences make sense. Colour the board. Play the game!

Number of players:
____

What you need:
coloured ________
a coin

Rules:
1 Toss the coin to move. Heads = 1, tails = 2.
2 If you land on an egg you __________ turn.
3 First person to ______________ wins.

	You win the pancake race! Move forward ______ spaces.	You __________ __________ Miss a turn!
You give up chocolate for Lent. Have a free turn!	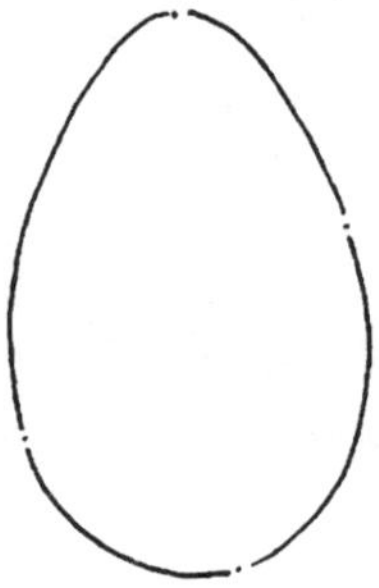	You bake a cake for Easter. Move forward______ __________ .
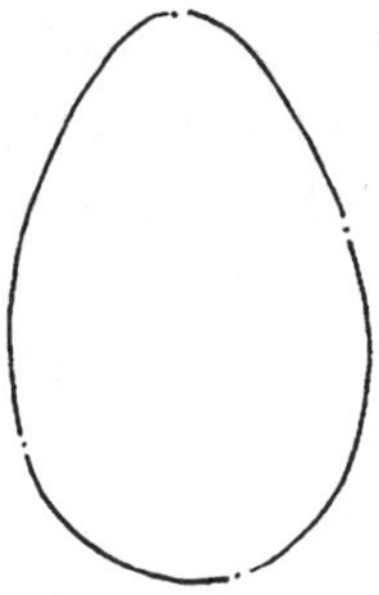	You make a lovely Easter card. You are safe!	You __________ __________ Miss a turn!
Your painted Easter egg wins first prize!____ __________	You __________ __________ Miss a turn!	

Things to do

Name ______________________

An Easter game

▲ You are going to make an Easter board game. Complete the instructions and rules. Complete each square on the board by writing information and/or instructions. Colour the board. Play the game!

Number of players: ______________ **What you need:** coloured ___________ a coin	**Rules:** 1 Toss the coin to move. Heads = 1, tails = 2. 2 If you land on an egg ____________________ . 3 To win you ______________________________ .

	You win the pancake race! Move forward __________ spaces.	
You give up chocolate for Lent. Have a free turn!		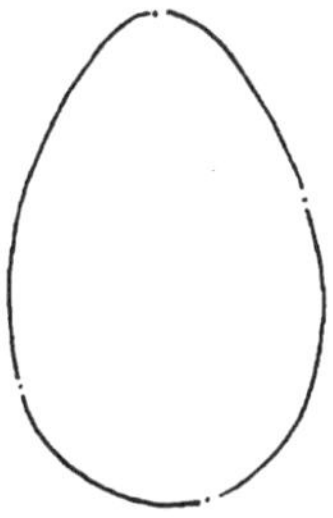
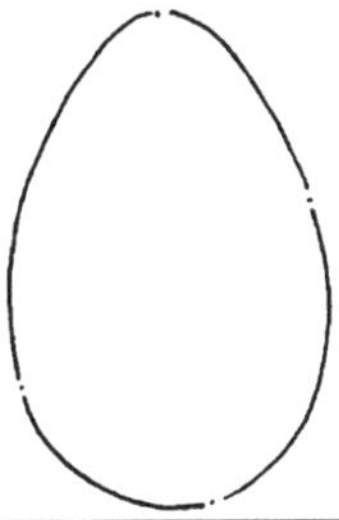		You burn the cake you made for Easter. Miss a turn.
You find two eggs in the egg hunt. ______________ ______________	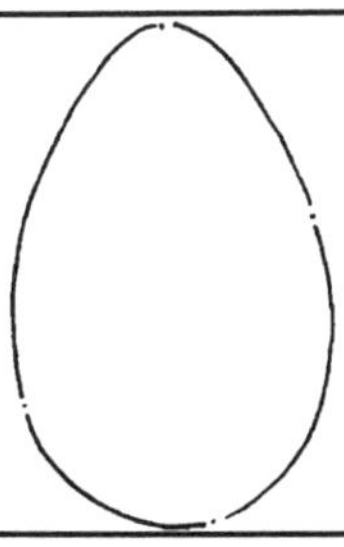	
	Your painted Easter egg wins first prize! You are safe!	

Things to do

Name ______________________

An Easter game

▲ You are going to make an Easter board game. First, make a set of 5 – 10 question cards about Easter with answers (use information books to help you). Decide on the rules for the game, including how the question cards will be used (ie what happens if you get it right, what happens if you get it wrong). Write out the rules. Write information and/or instructions on each square of the board. Colour the board. Play the game!

Rules:

1. Use a coin (not a die) to decide the number of moves. Heads = 1, tails = 2.
2. When you land on an egg, the other player picks up a question card. If you ______________________
3. ______________________
4. ______________________

	You make some lovely pancakes. Move forward 3 spaces.		**Question card**
You do not give up anything for Lent. Miss a turn!	**Question card**		
Question card		You bake a cake for Easter. Have a free turn.	**Question card**
		Question card	
Question card	Your painted Easter egg wins first prize! You are safe!		

Things to do

Name ____________________

Letter to the editor

▲ The editor of your local newspaper was sent this letter. She has to put in all the full stops and capital letters before it goes in the newspaper. Put them in for her.

5 bell street
oldtown
op4 7en

dear editor
i am writing this letter just before easter because i think parents should not buy easter eggs for their children this year
children eat far too many sweets today so they do not need any more
i think sweets should be banned
yours truly
mrs n well

▲ Now write a letter of your own to the editor about children eating sweets. Don't forget to use capital letters and full stops. Use the above letter and the words in the box to help you.

Dear Editor

Yours truly,

chocolate
enjoy
children
few
once
good
taste
nice
teeth
clean
dentist

Things to do

Name ______________________

Letter to the editor

▲ The editor of your local newspaper received this letter this week. Before the letter can be placed in the newspaper, she has to punctuate it. Put in all the full stops, capital letters, question marks (?), exclamation marks (!) and commas for the editor.

10 wellborn avenue
littletown
ln5 3 et

dear editor

i am writing just before easter in the hope that parents will read my letter and take notice of what i have to say i want to warn parents about the dangers of children eating too many sweets

when i was a child we only had sweets once a week because they were thought to be a special treat but what happens today today all children eat sweets on the way to school at school breaks after school and after their evening meal no wonder so many children today are putting on weight

i think parents should only give their children sweets once or twice a week they should be eating more fruit instead

at easter it gets worse the children eat so much chocolate they make themselves ill why do parents allow this to happen

so please take notice parents and try to look after the health of your children

yours sincerely

mrs j peters

▲ Write a letter to the editor in reply to this one. Tell the editor what your opinions are about children eating sweets. Do you agree or disagree with Mrs Peters?

▲ Write your letter on the back of this page. Make sure you punctuate it correctly!

Things to do

Name ______________________

Letter to the editor

▲ The editor of your local newspaper received this letter this week. Before it can be inserted in the newspaper, the editor has to punctuate it. Put in all the correct punctuation for her.

25 oak hill street
north youngtown
england
ny8 4or

dear editor

i am writing just before easter with a message of warning to all parents i wish to draw their attention to the health problems associated with the consumption of too many sweets

when i was a child we only had sweets once a week because they were considered to be special treats but what happens today today children eat sweets almost all day long they eat sweets morning noon and night on every day of the week

this high consumption creates a lot of health risks including weight gain skin problems and tooth decay do you want this to happen to your children yet all of these problems could be prevented through a better diet of more fruit and vegetables

so i urge you to consider your childrens health this easter and buy them a book or a game instead of an easter egg

yours sincerely

mr m lions

▲ Write a letter of your own to the editor in response to this one. Say whether you agree with Mr Lions or not. Write about your ideas on children eating sweets. Write your letter on the back of this page. Remember to check the punctuation carefully.

Things to do

Name ____________________

Making Easter eggs

▲ Read the writing below about how Easter eggs are made.

Chocolate is made from cocoa beans. First the cocoa beans are cleaned and then they are roasted. They are broken into small pieces which are crushed until they turn into a thick runny chocolate called mass. The mass is mixed with milk and sugar. It is then dried and crushed again. The mass has cocoa butter and flavourings added to it and then it is mixed again. The mixture is cooled to form chocolate. The chocolate is poured into an Easter egg mould to form two shells. The chocolate is cooled and the two shells are joined together to make an Easter egg.

▲ Now use what you have found out to complete this flow chart.

cocoa beans → c _ _ _ _ _ _ _ → r _ _ _ _ _ _ _ → broken into small pieces → c _ _ _ _ _ _ _ → mixed with milk and s _ _ _ _ → d _ _ _ _ → c _ _ _ _ _ _ _ → cocoa butter and flavourings are added → m _ _ _ _ → c _ _ _ _ _ _ → poured into an Easter egg mould → Easter egg

Things to do

Name ____________________

Making Easter eggs

▲ Read the information below. Use the information to complete the flow diagram.

Chocolate is made from cocoa beans. First the cocoa beans are cleaned and then they are roasted in revolving drums at 135 degrees celsius. The beans are then broken into small pieces. This is called kibbling. The next stage is winnowing where the outside shells of the beans are blown away by air currents. The beans are now called 'nibs'. The nibs are ground down until they turn into a thick liquid called 'mass'. The mass is mixed with milk and sugar and then it is dried to form 'crumb'. The crumb is ground down further and mixed with cocoa butter and flavourings. The mixture is mixed and beaten again (called 'conching') and then further mixing and cooling (tempering) forms the chocolate. The chocolate is poured into Easter egg moulds to form single shells. Two shells are then joined together to make the Easter egg.

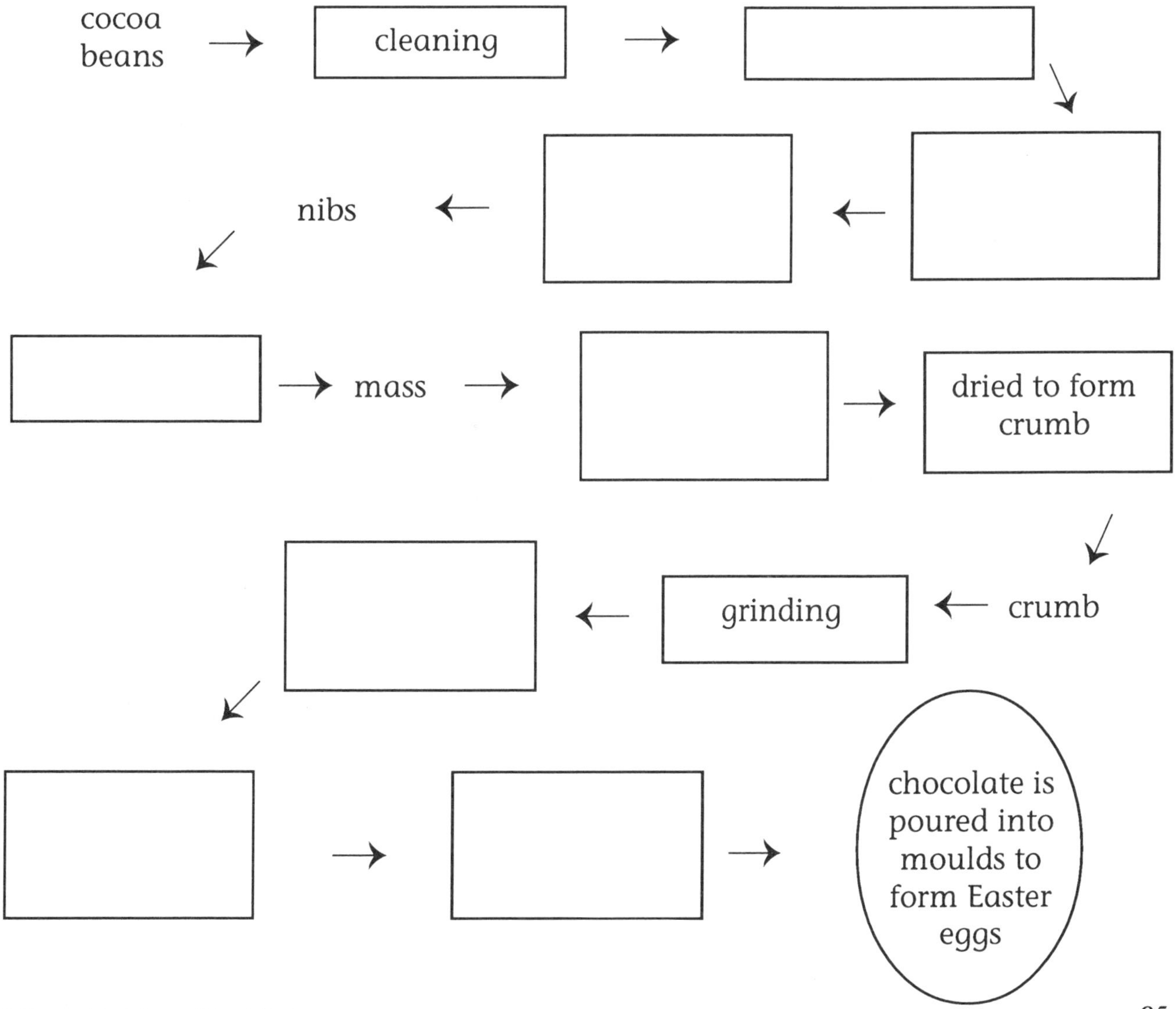

Things to do

Name ______________________

Making Easter eggs

▲ You are going to write a flow diagram of how Easter eggs are made. Read the information below and decide which parts of the information refer to the stages in the manufacture of Easter eggs. Then use these facts to draw and label your flow diagram.

Chocolate is made from cocoa beans. Cocoa is grown in many tropical rainforest regions throughout the world. On the cocoa trees grow many pods about 20 cm long. Inside the pod are about 40 seeds which are dried to produce the cocoa beans. The beans are then sold to chocolate factories.

At the factory, the cocoa beans are cleaned and then they are roasted in revolving drums at 135 degrees celsius. The beans undergo 'kibbling' where they are broken up into small pieces. The next stage is winnowing where the outside shells of the beans are blown away by air currents. The beans are now called 'nibs'. The nibs are ground down in steel pin mills until they turn into a thick chocolate-coloured liquid called 'mass'. The mass is mixed with milk and sugar and then it is dried to form 'crumb'. The crumb is pulverised and mixed with cocoa butter and flavourings. The mixture is mixed and beaten again (called 'conching') and then further mixing and cooling (tempering) forms the chocolate.

The chocolate is poured into Easter egg moulds to form single shells. Two shells are then joined together to make the Easter egg.

▲ Draw and label your flow diagram here: